T0110917

Also by Susan Marie Schulhof

Fun4Babies
Riding Waves
Living Red (Book 1 Suppression Series)

Little Stone House On the Corner

MAKE YOUR DREAMS COME TRUE

SUSAN MARIE SCHULHOF

BALBOA.PRESS

A DIVISION OF HAY HOUSE

Copyright © 2023 Susan Marie Schulhof.

All rights reserved. No part of this book may be used or reproduced by any means, graphic, electronic, or mechanical, including photocopying, recording, taping or by any information storage retrieval system without the written permission of the author except in the case of brief quotations embodied in critical articles and reviews.

This is a work of fiction. All of the characters, names, incidents, organizations, and dialogue in this novel are either the products of the author's imagination or are used fictitiously.

Balboa Press books may be ordered through booksellers or by contacting:

Balboa Press
A Division of Hay House
1663 Liberty Drive
Bloomington, IN 47403
www.balboapress.com
844-682-1282

Because of the dynamic nature of the Internet, any web addresses or links contained in this book may have changed since publication and may no longer be valid. The views expressed in this work are solely those of the author and do not necessarily reflect the views of the publisher, and the publisher hereby disclaims any responsibility for them.

The author of this book does not dispense medical advice or prescribe the use of any technique as a form of treatment for physical, emotional, or medical problems without the advice of a physician, either directly or indirectly. The intent of the author is only to offer information of a general nature to help you in your quest for emotional and spiritual well-being. In the event you use any of the information in this book for yourself, which is your constitutional right, the author and the publisher assume no responsibility for your actions.

Any people depicted in stock imagery provided by Getty Images are models, and such images are being used for illustrative purposes only. Certain stock imagery © Getty Images.

Print information available on the last page.

ISBN: 979-8-7652-4404-3 (sc)
ISBN: 979-8-7652-4403-6 (e)

Library of Congress Control Number: 2023913929

Balboa Press rev. date: 08/02/2023

This book is dedicated to my mother, Barbara, who taught me about the power of my soul and the universe. Her guidance has helped me navigate some of the most challenging times of my life and also encouraged me to pursue my dreams.

I HAD BIG DREAMS when I was a little girl, but life got in the way. I went to college but could not find a career I enjoyed. I got married and had three daughters, but I got divorced. I started dating again, but I never found someone to share the rest of my life with. Then I found a job and career that I liked, but it did not pay well. I studied religion, psychology, and spirituality, but I still struggled to live the life of my dreams. One day, I stopped fighting and resisting. I learned to surrender and listen. Slowly, my life is becoming the life that little girl hoped for.

It did not happen overnight, and I can't say it is an easy journey, but the life I am creating brings me such joy. This feeling of joy is not always synonymous with happiness; instead, it is an ongoing thought of satisfaction, an emotion of gratitude, and a sense of purpose. I want to share the steps I followed to change my life, narrated within a short story to help illustrate the process.

If there was a book that gave you steps to make your dream come true, would you read it? Would you follow the steps laid out on the pages? Are you ready to find YOUR little stone house? The way to make your dreams come true is simply to BEGIN.

Believing *is a simple task that takes much effort.*
Examine *your heart and your life to see what you really desire.*
Gratitude *is where life begins and ends.*
Intentions *create reality.*
Now *is the moment. Live in this truth, not in the past or in the future.*

*"**Believing** is a simple task that takes much effort."*

Sunday, March 22

As I glance over at the little stone house on the corner, I see the tip of a yellow daffodil just barely peeking out of the dirt. The tan stone bricks are weathered and worn, but the house looks cared for. I have only visited my Aunt Elsa and Uncle Riyen's place a few times since Aunt Elsa moved back to Walton about three years ago.

"Okay, Mom, I am here. Yes, I will keep an open mind and call you when I leave," I agree as I hang up the phone and fix my lipstick.

"What have I got myself into?" I think as I get out of my car and feel a cool breeze. I wish it were warmer so that I could have driven out here to the suburbs with the top down on my car. I don't have that many opportunities to drive on an open road without traffic since I live in the city. I put a smile on my face as I walk up the stairs and knock, noticing that my nail color matches the dark red door.

"Hi, Aunt Elsa," I say as I reach over to give her a hug as the door opens.

"Come in, come in. Let me take your coat," she offers as I step in.

We take a short walk through the family room and into the kitchen as Aunt Elsa says, "I know that you have been here before, but I can show you around after we have some tea. Is that okay? How long can you stay?"

"Of course, that's fine. I can stay a couple of hours. Ryan and I have dinner plans, but not until later tonight," I find myself responding even though my plan was to be in and out quickly. Although it is the weekend, I also have a lot of work to catch up on before we go to dinner.

"How do you like your tea, Tara?"

"A little sugar and milk," I answer, even though I am more of a coffee drinker. I see a couple of painted floral teacups and saucers set out on the dark wood table alongside some mini-sandwiches. It is such a nice display set out for me just coming over for tea. I wish I had more time to entertain like this. Most of the time, Ryan and I eat out or have a quick bite watching TV before falling exhausted into bed each night. When I was a little girl, I imagined a life where I could make a real difference in the world, but most days now, I wonder if what I do even matters. Ryan is a lawyer and works long hours at his job also. We often talk about what our life will be like one day when we have children and have time to live the life we want.

I sit down as I hear the blue and white, stripped teapot whistle. I watch as Elsa carefully pours us each a cup of tea. "So, how is Uncle Riyen?" I ask since I don't see him anywhere.

"He is wonderful; he went out to a movie so that we could have our little tea party," she explains so sweetly that I can just sense how much she loves him.

"I am so glad that you and him met. He is a very kind and thoughtful person."

"Me too. Before I met him, I had really given up on being in love. I mean, over the years, I did fall in love, or so I thought, but with no one that I could imagine spending my life with. I always wanted to, though," she says, sort of lost in her memories.

"Really? I thought all that you wanted was a life of adventure, seeing new places, and traveling the world."

"I did love seeing the world, and I still intend to see more of it, but I always wanted to have that one special person to share it with."

"And now you do," I add.

"That is right, which leads me to why I wanted you to come here. I know your mother told you that I want you to move to the suburbs, but I need to explain to you, myself, why exactly," she starts. I struggle to stay focused since I only came here to discuss this to appease my mom. My parents, Michael and Sophia, grew up in the suburbs and barely like driving to the city to visit us, so I know they hope we move.

Ryan and I have no desire to move to the suburbs, though. We love living in the city. There is so much action with so much to do all of the time. Although I must admit that lately, we are too tired from work that we end up staying in most nights.

"Your Uncle Riyen and I talked this over, and we feel that it is time to move out of this house. We want you and Ryan to move in here," explains my Aunt Elsa. She is my mother's younger sister and was always described as a free spirit with a strong mind of her own. As I listen to her speak, I notice her wavy blond hair is up in a loose bun, and she is wearing a flowing skirt with some sort of print and a black shirt. When she was younger, she traveled all over the world looking for adventures, so she wasn't around that much when I was young. Then when her mother, my grandmother, died a couple of years ago, she moved home to help care for her father. When he died shortly after, everyone thought that she would head back out traveling the world again, but instead, she bought this little house and stayed. Then she met my Uncle Riyen, who is the yin to her yang, so to speak. I wondered if both of them want to go traveling or why would they want to sell their home?

"That's sweet, Aunt Elsa, but don't you and Uncle Riyen want to stay in your own home? You guys haven't lived here that long; why would you want to move?"

"This is more than a home, Tara; this is a special house. It is a little house on the corner made of simple stone where extraordinary things happen to those who live here," states Aunt Elsa as if she was reading it, but then she quietly adds, "It makes dreams come true." Although Tara would agree that her aunt and uncle have a great life, she wasn't sure if the house was special. It was charming and so very unique, but how could a simple stone house make people's dreams come true?

"It is a beautiful little house, but I just don't know," I respond as I glance around the little kitchen. I can tell that it has recently been remodeled, and now that I really look, I see that all of the appliances look brand new and seem to be state of the art.

"Oh Tara, I just fell in love with this house the moment I walked in the front door. I still love it, but this house is a gift that must be passed on to others, or it will stop working."

"Hmm, that's so interesting," I reply, not sure how to respond to the bizarre twist in this conversation, not wanting to insult her. We have grown closer in the last couple of years since she returned to Walton, but I still don't know her that well. I wonder if my mom knows that Elsa believes this house can make dreams come true.

"I know it seems hard to believe. I was skeptical at first, too," she explains as if reading my mind.

I just nod since I don't know what to say. We sit in silence for so long that I think that maybe it is time for me to leave, so I stand up to clear my teacup.

"How are the fertility tests going? Is the doctor any closer to understanding why you are not getting pregnant?" Aunt Elsa asks cautiously.

"Not really. The good news is they can't seem to find anything wrong with Ryan or with me, but it's just not happening," I answer without turning back to the table, as a tear fills my eye, thinking about how we have been trying for so many years to have a baby. My hand starts to shake as I set the cup on the counter by the sink. Since I met Ryan at college, and we both wanted to get established in our careers, our time for having children is almost passing us by. I always thought when I was ready to get pregnant that it would just happen, but it hasn't. We have tried so many things but with no success. The next step is in-vitro, but that takes time and money. Although we are fortunate to have the money to try it, I just keep thinking that it will happen on it's own since there seems to be nothing to indicate that it can't occur. I sit back down and look at Aunt Elsa.

"I am sorry to ask about such a personal situation, but your mom is so worried about you, and as you know, she is anxious to become a Grandma," she adds with a chuckle.

"That's okay. Even complete strangers ask us when we are going to start a family. It makes me think about how difficult that is for people who have things wrong or even how it feels for people who don't want to have children. Since we are being so open, did you want to have kids?" I ask cautiously.

"I did when I was young, but my love of traveling was even more important to me. Plus, I never found someone I connected so strongly with until your Uncle Riyen, of course, but by then, my days of having kids were long past."

"Uncle Riyen is so wonderful. I am glad that you met him," I say again. They are both around the same age, and neither has ever been married or had kids. Riyen's family came here from India, but he was born and raised here.

"Me too, but he is part of why I want you to move in here. There is so much to tell you, but I would like to meet with you and Ryan both together to explain the magic of this house."

"I am not sure when he could come. He works so much, as do I, so I am just not sure, Aunt Elsa," I stammer.

"I really wish that you could make it a priority to come for a couple of hours next weekend, honey. As I said, there is much to explain, but this house could help make your dream come true. It is truly a magical house. As I told you earlier, I loved to travel, and I wanted to find love when I was young. I thought that I could have both. I did meet people that I cared about, but never anyone I could really imagine a lifetime with. Then when your grandmother died, I knew that I needed to move home to help your grandfather. It was not fair to leave that burden on your mom when she had a husband and a career of her own, as well as you and your brother in her life."

"I remember how I loved hearing about all of your adventures growing up. I am glad that you moved back here, but I am sorry for the reasons."

"Oh, don't feel sorry. I stayed because I do love it here in Walton, and I did want to be near your mom, but there is more to it. I hoped to tell you and Ryan about this house together, but maybe you just need to hear my story first."

Slowly, she began telling me the story that led to buying this little stone house on the corner, and how she came to meet Uncle Riyen. When she finished, she had me convinced that this house helped her to meet and fall in love with Uncle Riyen. Her dream of finally finding the man she would marry came true because of this house, and she believes with all of her heart that if Ryan and I moved in here, our wish to have a baby could and would come true.

I thought about her story and life on the whole drive home. I am not sure how to convince Ryan to make this bold and spontaneous move, but I want to try and see if the magic of this house is true. For the first time in years, I see possibilities again. I didn't want to give up, but the pain of wanting what we didn't have was so overwhelming.

Ryan asks me about my visit to Aunt Elsa's the minute I get home because he knows how reluctant I was to drive to her house today. We knew that it had something to do with moving to the suburbs since my mom said that. One of the things that I love about him is how pragmatic he is, so I know that I need to figure out how to convince him that this is a good plan for us to try. I decide to wait until we are at dinner, relaxed with our first glass of wine to explain to him how we could afford to buy this house from Elsa and Riyen while we rent out our place in the city.

Ryan has on black slacks with a dark green sweater, and just looking across the table at him reminds me how much I love him and want to have a baby that could have those light green eyes of his. I know that my dark brown eyes might win out, but since I am wishing for a child, I could wish for his eyes too. He has dark brown hair that is curly when he lets it grow a little longer, so he keeps it that perfect length, of not too short and not too long. He wears his glasses most of the time because he thinks his baby face keeps him from being taken seriously and respected in court, but I thought he was so handsome the first time I met him. It didn't take long before I fell in love with his sweet soul.

The waiter brings our wine, and while we wait for our meals, I decide to just dive in. I am unsure why I feel so nervous; I usually never feel this way with Ryan. Since the day that we met, we have been able to talk about anything, and surprisingly, we usually agree. The one area in which we may be differ is talking about spiritual matters. I grew up in a home that was more open to ideas of mystical occurrences. My Grandmother, Claire, had her own set of Tarot cards, but she never pushed it on my brother and me. My mother does believe in astrology and tarot cards also, but I guess I have never shared their interest, so I do not know that much about it. Sure, I have seen the psychics on television and do find it interesting, but I have never gone to one myself.

"So, I am not sure what your plans are next weekend, but I really would like us to talk to my Aunt Elsa together," I start off.

"If it's important to you, of course, I can make time, but I thought you just went to see her because your mother encouraged you to go. Was it about us moving out of the city?"

"I did, and yes, but there is just so much to explain about the house that I think Elsa could tell you better. She and Uncle Riyen actually want us to move into their house."

"Wow, why? I know your mother wants us to move closer to her, but why their house? Where are they moving?" Ryan asks as he raises his eyebrow at me.

"It's complicated, but the short story is that Aunt Elsa believes her house is magical and can help make our dream of having a baby come true," I blurt out, "I am not sure if my mother knows that part."

Ryan takes a sip of his wine as he looks questioningly at me.

"I know, I know, that's what I thought when Aunt Elsa said it to me as we were drinking our tea, but I don't know, when she told me her story about moving there and wishing for love and then meeting Uncle Riyen, it just seemed possible."

"You know I love you, Tara, but I don't believe that a simple house could hold that power," he says as the waiter brings our food, the rigatoni for me and eggplant parmesan for Ryan. We are both quiet as we start to eat.

Finally, Ryan speaks first, "If you want me to go hear about this magic house next weekend, we will, but I can't make any promises. I like our place and our life here in the city, plus I don't believe in things I can't explain."

"Thank you, Ryan. I don't know how to explain it, but for the first time in awhile, I feel hopeful, like maybe we can have a family."

"We are a family already, Tara, but I know that you mean with a baby."

"Or even a couple of babies," I chuckle as I clink my glass against his, wondering how I can convince him to move there while everything my Aunt Elsa told me about today replays in my mind.

Saturday, March 28

Ryan turns to me with that one raised eyebrow as he pulls up to the little stone house. I smile at him nervously as I open the car door and see that more daffodils are coming through the dirt but not yet blooming. Ryan said he would come to listen, but I think he agreed just so that he could tell them no thank you for the offer to buy the place. I take his hand as we walk to the front door and knock. As my Uncle Riyen opens it, he welcomes us in.

"Elsa, Tara and Ryan are here," he shouts as my Aunt Elsa emerges from the kitchen wearing an apron.

"It smells delicious in here," I say as I give them both a hug.

"I made some butternut squash soup for us," she says as we sit down in the family room, "First, we will talk, and then we can eat, okay?"

"Okay," Ryan and I both say.

"So, how was the drive here?" asks Uncle Riyen.

"It was smooth, hardly any traffic," responds Ryan, "Although it is the weekend, so traffic is usually better coming this way."

"I know that Tara told you about our wish for you to buy this house from us, but please hear us out before you make your decision," starts Aunt Elsa after some silence.

We both nod as she begins to tell Ryan the story of how she had traveled the world but also wished for love all of her life, for someone to share her life with. Even though we had heard the story before, Elsa explained to us about moving back home when her mother died and then how her father died. She continued explaining how she bought this house and then the story of meeting Riyen. Everything she was telling Ryan, I had heard last weekend until she got to the part about meeting someone at the library and how she came upon this little stone house.

"So there I was at the library researching ideas for my next book when this woman just came up to me and said that she remembered me from college. We spoke for a while, catching up on each other's lives, but honestly, I did not remember her at all. She looked to be about the same age as me, so it was possible. Anyway, I told her about my parents' deaths and how I was selling their house, so I could go back on the road traveling and writing when she told me that she lived in this amazing little stone house on a corner that was very special. She was very persuasive and invited me over for tea the next day to show me the house. I was so curious that even though I couldn't remember her, I still agreed to go. The next day as we were having tea, she told me how the house made her dream of becoming a doctor come true."

"Didn't she just go to medical school to become a doctor?" Ryan says but without a trance of sarcasm.

"Yes, of course. Can I get you something to drink before I explain?"

We both respond that we would like a glass of water, so Uncle Riyen gets a pitcher and four glasses as Aunt Elsa waits to continue.

"As you asked, she did need to take the steps to apply and go to medical school, but she explained that no one in her family had even gone to college, let alone became a doctor. Her parents were proud that she went to school and became a registered nurse, but no one encouraged her or believed that she could make it though medical school. Plus, thinking about the enormous burden to pay for it just made her even more convinced that she shouldn't go. However, she saved up enough money and bought this house. She didn't explain how she found out about the house or how this house helped her exactly, but she was insistent that it is magical. When she asked me what my dream was, I don't know why, but I confided in her that all I really wanted was to find someone to share my life with. All she said was that she knew it the minute she saw me at the library, and that is why she wanted me to have this house."

I glance over at Ryan. He seems to be listening, but his face doesn't give any indication of what he is thinking about any of this. The more I hear, though, the more I want to move here, to this house. I look around the room as she speaks, trying to imagine our life here. Our furniture might be newer and a little more modern than Elsa and Riyen's, but I begin to visualize each piece of our furniture here. I think that it will all fit. Our place in the city is small since everything costs more downtown. I know from last week that it has a small un-finished basement with two bedrooms and one and a half bathrooms along with the kitchen and the family room. Even though this place is small, it has a high vaulted ceiling in this room and beautiful hardwood floors all through it. I am not sure if Elsa and Riyen put them in, but I can tell that it has been taken care of.

"Do we want to take a break and show Ryan the house?" I ask hopefully.

"Yes," replies Aunt Elsa.

"That is a good idea," adds Uncle Riyen.

As they show us around, he explains all the improvements he and Elsa have made to the house in the short year that he lived here after they got married.

"It is clear to me that you both love this house; why do you want to sell it?" Ryan asks.

"That's a trick question," laughs Elsa, "We don't really want to move, but we know that this house is a gift that should be given to others. We know that we might not be able to find a new house that we would love as much, but we really want you two to live here."

Everyone is silent as we look at the rest of the house and then sit back down in the family room. As Uncle Riyen goes to refill the water pitcher and our glasses, Aunt Elsa goes and gets a tattered old brown leather book and some envelopes.

"This is how we know that this house is magic," explains Aunt Elsa as she hands Ryan the book and just one envelope. As he undoes the tie and opens the small brown book, all we see are dates and people's names listed. As we scan the book, we realize that it contains a list, a very long list, of dates that people lived in this house with their names and descriptions of their dreams and how they came true. As I lean close to Ryan and we look at page after page, I find myself wondering how long ago this house was built and simultaneously thinking about how soon we can move in. I still can't tell by Ryan's expression how he is taking all of this information.

"Do we open the envelope?" I ask as I look at the front of it and see it is labeled *"One: Believing is a simple task that takes much effort."*

"The question is not whether you open it, but it is should you open it? Believing in this house is the first and most important step. You can have concerns and be skeptical, but do you believe that this is possible?" Aunt Elsa asks.

"I do believe it is possible, but what about you, Ryan?" I ask with such trepidation in my voice.

"I definitely have my reservations, but something inside of me is urging me to believe. This house just feels so much like a home. I never realized until today how impersonal our place in the city feels. I might regret this, but yes, I think we should open the envelope," Ryan explains as he hands me the envelope to open. After I open the clasp, I slide my fingers in, pulling out a simple sheet of weathered paper with words on them. I begin to read aloud.

Congratulations on embarking on an amazing adventure. This little stone house contains the remarkable power to make your dreams come true. The first step is often the most difficult, but be proud, for you have decided to take it. This is not a genie-in-the-bottle-type house. In order to manifest your dreams, you will need to believe, as well as trust, and take the necessary steps along the way. You cannot move to the next envelope, step two, until you are living here. Now as you prepare for and complete the task of moving into this special house, remember that believing is a simple task that takes much effort. As it will be with all six steps, you cannot read ahead; each envelope must only be opened when the current exercise is completed, and you must not tell others what these envelopes say unless and until it is their turn to have their dreams come true.

"But how will we know when to open the next envelope?" I ask.

"I worried about that too, but you will know when the right time is. Don't worry," Aunt Elsa answers.

"So when we rent out or sell our place and move here, where will you go?" Ryan asks Aunt Elsa and Uncle Riyen.

"No need to worry about us. We will move out soon, so the house will be ready whenever you can move in. Your Aunt Elsa and I have some plans in the works," Uncle Riyen says.

I am excited and scared all at once. I can't believe that Ryan agreed to do this, especially so quickly, but I am so grateful. Every fiber of my being is telling me that we need to do this. I do start to get nervous when I think about how much longer Ryan's and my commute to work each day will be, and I am not even sure how we will find the time to move our belongings and rent out our place, but I want to believe.

"We can talk more about the details as we eat. Anyone ready for some soup?" Aunt Elsa asks, "I made it this morning, and Riyen baked some fresh bread for us too."

As I grab Ryan's hand and we walk into the kitchen, all that I can think about is that soon this home will be ours, and if everything is true, maybe by this time next year, Ryan and I could have a baby of our own.

After a few more hours of eating and figuring out the logistics of buying the house, we climb into our car to head home. Ryan hasn't said a word, so I worry that he is having second thoughts, but then he says, "So should we stop and get some boxes on our way home? I think it might be easy to find a renter for our place, and since Elsa and Riyen are putting their stuff in storage to go to Australia traveling, they should be moving out soon, huh?"

"Yes, let's start packing tonight," I say as I turn toward Ryan and smile.

Saturday, April 18

I put the last of my belongings in my bag as I walk through our place, thinking that we must be crazy as well as desperate to be doing this. Only Aunt Elsa and Uncle Riyen know exactly why we are doing this. People from work and even our family look at us with astonishment that we are actually moving from our home in the city. Since most people just know we are moving but not the story behind it, they probably think we are having some kind of life crisis. I vacillate each day between believing and doubting, but I know that I need just to have faith.

"That is it. The movers have everything on the truck," Ryan says.

"We can come back through tomorrow to clean and make sure we didn't forget anything," I reply, even though we have been packed and ready to move for the last four days.

I am surprised at how quickly we were able to pack everything and find someone to rent this place. The law firm Ryan works at just hired a new lawyer. She and her husband are moving here and need a place to rent until they decide where they will settle down permanently, so it was perfect timing since they needed to find a place quickly. Aunt Elsa and Uncle Riyen left yesterday for their adventure in Australia. Since he never really traveled before, Uncle Riyen was so nervous when we said goodbye, but since my Aunt Elsa spent most of her life traveling, I knew he would have fun. My parents are ecstatic because we will be living closer to them now, plus it is easier to come to the house than to drive to where we lived in the city and find parking. Except for that first night, we haven't really talked about all that Elsa told us about the house. We both had so many questions about it, and we each admitted that we were very curious to open the other envelopes. It's probably a good thing the envelopes and the book stayed at Aunt Elsa's, or should I say our little stone house, because we both wanted to read them.

We have been back to the house to re-read the first envelope a few times and to measure for our furniture. Except for a couple of things that we will just store in the basement, we think everything is going to fit. Surprisingly, the house has a two-car garage, so both of ours will be inside. I took off a few days to give myself time to unpack before making the drive to the city for work. Ryan is going to try the train Monday since his office is right by a stop, but I would have a thirty-minute walk to my office if I took the train, so I am planning on driving.

"They are almost done securing the items on the truck, so we should head out to get there first," Ryan says as I take one last glance around.

Since we left my car there yesterday, we go down the elevator and got in Ryan's SUV. Ryan will bring the keys to Sarah and her husband on Monday so that they can move into the place we have called home for five years. I thought I might be sad leaving here, but my excitement over the possibilities overshadow any fear and sadness I have.

As we head to the suburbs, I notice that spring has really arrived since all of the trees are starting to sprout leaves. We turn the corner to our new house, I notice that the front is covered in a layer of daffodils in full bloom, welcoming us. All of my worry and trepidation evaporate as I see the yellow glow around the little stone house on the corner that we will now call home.

Once we park the car and walk around to the front, Ryan turns to me and says, "Welcome to our new home."

He kisses me and pulls me into his arms. He surprises me as he lifts me up and carries me across the threshold. His excitement reassures me that we made the right decision moving here. I am ready to open the next envelope and begin this adventure. I really do believe in the magic of this little stone house.

Once the movers have unpacked the truck and we are working on the kitchen, we realize that we forgot to have dinner. We order a pizza and then go to set up the bedroom before we get too tired. After eating and both taking quick showers, we collapse onto the bed. I reach over and grab Ryan's hand exhausted.

"I can't believe how quickly and smoothly everything went with moving here," Ryan says, pulling me into a hug.

I reply with a slight chuckle, "I know; it feels like magic."

"It does," he replies, holding me tighter, "But remember that whatever happens, we are already a family."

"I agree," I say, adding, "It doesn't feel like the right time to open the second envelope."

"I thought the same thing, Tara. Even though I am anxious to read it, how about we just read the first envelope again before falling asleep?" Ryan asks as he reaches over to the side table where he puts the tattered book and envelopes. He hands the first envelope to me and chuckles, "It is your turn to read, which is good since I am too tired to keep my eyes open."

"I can't believe we really did this," I say as I open the envelope and begin to read aloud.

"Now, as you prepare for and complete the task of moving into this special house, remember that believing is a simple task that takes much effort," we both say together. I kiss Ryan as I turn off the light. We just look at each other as we lay in bed, ready to go to sleep in our little stone house on the corner.

"**Examine** your heart and your life
to see what you really desire."

Sunday, April 19

"Are you ready?" I ask Ryan as we sit at our kitchen table eating breakfast. The kitchen isn't completely organized, but it already feels like home. It is painted a light yellow that I initially thought we might change, but it looks nice with our furniture in here. It feels like a great place to start the day. The rest of the house is painted in neutral shades, so our stuff looks perfect.

"Yes," he says as he looks up at me with a smile.

I have been thinking about that second envelope since I woke up, but as Aunt Elsa said about knowing when the time was right to open it, it didn't feel right until now. I walk into the bedroom and bring the second envelope with the words *"Two: Examine your heart and your life to see what you really desire"* on it, and sit back down across from Ryan. It is very tempting to read the front of each envelope, but I want to do this right.

"So this envelope says 'Examine your heart and your life to see what you really desire' on the front of it," I say as Ryan looks expectantly at me, "I think that you should read this one, Ryan. I am too nervous, okay?"

"Of course," he says as he takes the envelope from me and opens the clasp revealing another worn piece of paper. Then he begins to read.

Congratulations on completing the first step of this adventure. Your next step, step two, is to examine your heart and your life to see what you really desire. Remember that this little stone house contains the remarkable power to make your dreams come true, but in order to manifest your dreams, you will need to continue to believe, as well as now, you must also take the necessary steps along the way. You cannot move to the next envelope, step three, until at least, if not more than, one month from today. I know that you are anxious and feel confident that you

15

know clearly what your dream is, but over this month or longer, if needed, you must spend time in self-reflection and deep awareness of the life you are living and the choices you are making. You must examine your heart and your life to see what you really desire. Experiences in life without examination can rarely offer meaning or purpose. You will determine if your dream is really in alignment with your life, your choices, and your actions. There are a series of questions and tasks that you must do over this month, so please read each carefully and take each one seriously. Remember also, as it will be with all steps, you cannot read ahead; each envelope must only be opened when the current exercise is completed, and you must not tell others what these envelopes say unless and until it is their turn to have their dreams come true.

I have to admit that I am disappointed that we can't open the next envelope for a month or maybe even longer. As I question what we got ourselves into, I am tempted to just open envelope three and see what the next step is. I already know that my dream is to be a mother, so why do I need to answer these questions and do these tasks? Ryan re-reads the page silently as I slowly feel sadness creep over me, thinking that this is stupid.

"I know this is hard, and you are anxious to open the next envelope," Ryan starts, "But believing does take much effort."

"I know, but I just want to become a mother. If every step takes this long, I just don't know…." I begin to cry without finishing.

"I love you, honey," Ryan whispers as he holds me.

"I wanted to have a baby by this time next year, though," I say through my sobs.

"And we might still. We have waited this long; let's just do this right, Tara."

When I finally stopped crying, we read through the five items on the list in envelope two.

Over the next month, or however long it takes to complete these five items, you will examine your heart and life to determine your true desires.

- *List three things that you would make come true if you could today.*
- *List two ways/actions (under each of the three things above) that you have taken to achieve this thing.*

- *Reflect on this process. Become aware of your wishes and actions of each one. Look back at the experience for connection and learning. "That was an amazing experience," or "I didn't handle that they way that I wanted to." Focus on your feelings as you reflect on an experience, person, or situation. Learn from it so that you don't repeat things you didn't handle well.*
- *Determine if the dream, or wish, you say that you want to come true, is at the top of your list right now. Is there another wish you want first or more? Examine if there are other steps you could still take toward all of your wishes.*
- *Write out a detailed description of what your day-to-day life would look like if this dream came true. As you reflect on this, see where your focus was. Did you feel excited, anxious, or hopeful? Were you dreading parts of it? Did you feel sad, mad, happy, surprised, or scared?*

As we resume unpacking, neither of us brings up the list of to-do items. After lunch, Ryan suggests going for a walk. I wash my face and pull my brown hair into a high ponytail as we head out the door. Ryan loves working out, but I am more of a reader in my free time. I wonder if, now that we live in the suburbs, I will walk more. I love the street we live on since each of the houses look so different and unique. Some houses had been torn down, with newer and bigger ones replacing them, but many look like the original house.

"As I unpacked today, I thought that maybe it would be good if we each came up with the answer to the first question separately. I know that we both want the same thing, to have a baby, but let's see what other two things we each come up with, if we could make it come true today?" Ryan suggests while we are walking.

"I don't have three things though; I just have the one thing, Ryan," I say as we turn the corner leaving our street.

"Seriously, Tara? We have known each other for a long time. You have always been driven to achieve and be the best. There must be something else you would make come true if you could?"

"What about you? Are you saying there are other things besides having a baby that you want?" I ask curiously.

"Yes," he says cautiously as he stops and looks at me, "You know that I have always wanted a dog. Growing up, my parents never let me

17

have one, and then once I started my career, it didn't seem fair to get a dog when neither of us was home very much. Think about this walk with a dog and how much fun it would be."

"I knew you wanted one, but I suppose I didn't realize how much you wanted one. Okay, I will try to stop being upset that this step could take so long. I guess if I am being honest, I would love to be able to have more balance at work and maybe even be able to work from home some days."

"So, three things that we each would make come true today if we could? Let's see if we can come up with those by tonight, and we can talk about it before bed."

"Sounds like a plan," I say as I stop walking and give Ryan a kiss.

"I love you, Tara."

"I love you too, Ryan."

Saturday, April 25

"Good morning, honey," I say as I pad into the kitchen barefoot, where Ryan is doing work already this morning.

"I made some eggs if you want some," Ryan tells me and angles his head toward the stovetop without looking up from his computer.

"Thanks," I say as I make myself a cup of coffee and get some eggs.

We both came up with the three things we would make come true if we could, pretty easily last Sunday once I let go of my frustration. However, to come up with two actions that we have taken to achieve them is challenging. My three things were to have a baby, have more flexibility in my work, and to go on a vacation. Ryan's were very similar like wanting a baby and going on a vacation, plus then wanting a dog as well. It seems funny that we both wanted a vacation, but neither of us told the other one. I always thought that one of the things that brought us together was our work and our success-driven personalities, so I guess it makes sense that neither of us expressed that we needed a break from work.

For action steps, we have been trying to get pregnant and have read pregnancy and fertility books. In addition, we went to doctors and to specialists to see if there was a reason that I couldn't get pregnant, so after reflection, we decided that were trying to make that desire happen and that it definitely was at the top of our list. What about our other ones? Did that wish to become pregnant occupy so much of our thoughts that we couldn't see anything else?

"So what would it take for us to go on that vacation we both want?" I ask.

"I don't know," replies Ryan as he shuts his laptop, "Where would you even want to go? Like, what kind of vacation are you thinking?"

"Somewhere relaxing with no work allowed," I laugh," And then when we get back, maybe we can look at getting a dog?"

"Are you serious?" Ryan smiles.

"I talked to Molly about the possibility of working from home some days, so that would help if we had a dog at home. I also asked about taking some time off to go on vacation next week. She said yes to both and even wondered why I never take vacations."

"I asked about taking time off too, which is why I am working already today. As soon as I finish this case which should be by the end of this week, I asked to not have another assigned until we get back," he laughs.

"Well, that was easier than we thought," I say as I get up and sit on his lap.

"So now we need to figure out where to go in a week," he says.

"A beach, or maybe hiking somewhere?"

"Let me ask my mom about the place in Florida she goes to. Maybe we could rent it? It would be beautiful this time of year, and it is right on the Gulf of Mexico?"

After Ryan calls his mom, and she tell him that she will look into renting the place in Florida, we both do a little more work. Then we spend the afternoon looking up different breeds of dogs. Since neither of us know how to or have a desire to have a garden, we realize that we can turn the small-enclosed area into a dog run since the back door leads directly into it. I can't remember the last time I saw Ryan's eyes light up as much as they did talking about getting a dog. I keep trying to remind him how much work having a dog would be, but all he can see is the joy of finally having his own pet. My pragmatic husband has put on his rose-colored glasses when it comes to having a dog.

Monday, May 4

It is our third day of vacation, and now two weeks after we read envelope two. We reflected on our dreams and actions, but we still haven't finished this envelope. It's funny that I usually am a "cross things off my list type of person," but we still haven't completed the last step-- *Write out a detailed description of what your day-to-day life would look like if this dream came true.*

I have thought about it a lot because it is difficult to imagine how much our lives would change if we had a baby and a dog. Obviously, since I am sitting on a balcony in a condo in Florida watching the sun set over the water, I can't even imagine this wish coming true and what I would be doing instead. I started working from home one day a week, so that wish I can picture, but I still haven't figured out the concept of owning a dog and what that would really be like. I definitely want to be realistic when we complete this step, and be specific when we need to write it out. How will a baby and a dog fit into our busy life?

"Have you thought about the last step we need to do, Ryan?" I ask as I take a sip of my wine.

"Yes, all the time. As much as I want a baby and a dog, too, I am glad we took this vacation together now. It's hard to imagine being here with a baby."

"I was just thinking the same thing; I don't know why we didn't do this sooner."

"I know. What were we waiting for?" Ryan says as he sips his wine, "Should we work on writing it out tonight?"

"How about tomorrow since I am ready for another glass of wine as we watch this beautiful sky change colors?" I answer.

"Want to go walk down by the water tonight to watch?"

"Good idea," I reply as I get up, and we walk in from the patio.

It feels so good to lean back on Ryan as the sun drops below the horizon. The first couple of days were difficult to get out of my work mindset and stop thinking about what I need to do, but today as we went to the pool and made dinner together, I realized how much we are missing out in life by working so much.

"I wonder if my company has paternity leave?" Ryan asks aloud but more to himself as we try to fall asleep.

We decide to go out for breakfast tomorrow and work on what our day-to-day life description would look like if our dream to have a baby came true. Since we are going to look at getting a dog when we get back, and I am already starting to work from home some days, those will also be part of our vision. As I try to sleep, I get stuck on who will take care of the baby while we work. Would one of us stay home? Would we hire a nanny or find childcare? Could either of our parents help by watching the baby one day a week? As I drift off with these questions in my mind, I realize that we never really talked about these things. We were just so focused on having a baby that we could not see the big picture.

Tuesday, May 5

"Morning honey," I say as I turn towards Ryan as he is reading a book in bed. I still can't get use to him relaxing since usually he is working or working out.

"Morning," he says as he kisses me.

"Have you been awake long?" I ask as I get up and head to the bathroom.

"No, just a little bit."

"Should I get ready to go to breakfast?"

"It's up to you, but we are on vacation, so we probably don't need to even hurry to go to breakfast unless you are really hungry?"

"No, I could read a little too, but I am going to make coffee. Want a cup?"

"Sure, thanks."

As I make our coffee, I think about what we would be doing if we had a baby here. Obviously, I probably wouldn't have slept in unless Ryan got up with the baby. The focus of our attention would be on the baby, not us, and especially not on work like it has been all of these years.

Wednesday, May 6

After writing out the rough draft description of what our day-to-day life would be like yesterday, we both realized that neither of us was being very realistic about life with a baby. Neither of us wanted to give up our career, but we both agreed to start cutting back on our hours at work now to prepare for a baby and a new dog. We are both going to talk to our parents about possibly helping with childcare or even just helping sometimes if the baby is sick. We also are going to ask around about a nanny versus childcare. I think we both are swaying towards childcare so that he or she can be with other kids and have more of an educational setting. We believe that there is a place near where our condo in the city is, but we can't decide where we want to live after having a baby since we are both enjoying our house in the suburbs more than we thought we would.

Once we get some of these decisions figured out, we need to work on our final description a little more. It's funny that the envelope directions said, "*...you must spend time in self-reflection and deep awareness of the life you are living and the choices you are making*" because I don't think either of us did this much reflection and thinking about our life and desires outside of our work goals before. I know that I figured that the first step was getting pregnant and then figuring this all out. As much as I want a baby, I am glad we have time to talk these things over and decide now without the pressure or emotions that come with a pregnancy.

I think the waitress was ready for us to leave yesterday since talking this over and trying to write out a detailed description took much longer than we anticipated. We decided to go for a swim and relax a little before diving back into the discussion today. We have the basic framework figured out, except for some of the details that we can look into after vacation.

"Want to work on our description out here by the pool?" I decide to ask.

"No, let's go in and get a snack before we start. I have been thinking about everything nonstop, so I would kind of like to get it finished, so we can really relax for the last few days here."

"I thought that too. Since there are some details about childcare that we still need to figure out when we go home, maybe we should just write up the final description of what life would be like with a dog and finish the baby one once we are home. I also wouldn't mind thinking about when we could plan another vacation too. It wouldn't need to be a whole week, but I don't want to get back into the work habits that we had before."

"I love how you are thinking," Ryan says with a huge smile on his face.

"I love you, ya know?" I say back.

"I love you too. So were you thinking of a puppy, or do we think about adopting an older dog?"

"Hmm, I never thought about it," I say as I stand up to head inside, "Most of the pictures and websites we were looking at online were puppies."

"Well, you better start thinking. That would be two different daily descriptions," Ryan chuckles, standing up too.

Saturday, May 30

After visiting my parents, I smile as I pull up to our little stone house on the corner. The daffodils are done blooming, but I still love the warm and welcoming feeling of home when I pull into the driveway.

"Ryan," I yell out back," Want to go for a walk with me?"

"Sure, can you wait twenty minutes? I am almost done," he asks.

"Okay, need help?" I ask since I know that he stayed home to work on the yard and the enclosed area that we are transforming into a dog-run area.

"No, but thank you."

I walk back in and get a glass of lemonade for myself and one for Ryan for when he is done. As I sit and look around the kitchen, I am once again surprised by how it feels like we have always lived here. Who would have believed that when I came to talk to my Aunt Elsa in March that two months later, we would be moved in and making it a home? In addition to both of us working less, me working from home one day a week and taking that glorious vacation to Florida. I miss sitting outside watching the sunsets, but I am trying to keep that feeling of calmness and relaxation in my evening and weekends.

"The dog run is ready," Ryan says as he walks in from the back, "How were your parents? Did you tell them what I was working on?"

"Yes, I think they think we are crazy getting a dog. My mom is worried that we won't want a baby anymore once we have the responsibility of a pet. I assured her that we still will. It's so weird keeping the magic of this house from her and everyone, but I know that the directions said we can only tell people who move in after us."

"It is hard, but at least you have your Aunt Elsa and Uncle Riyen to talk to now that they are home."

"In many ways, I feel like we are so different now," I say to Ryan as he sits down.

"I know what you mean," he says as I hand him the lemonade, "But in a good way, right?"

"Definitely," I say as I kiss him hard.

"Kiss me like that after our walk and my shower," he chuckles as a feeling of contentedness washes over me, and we head out the door.

Saturday, June 6

We almost have all of the details worked out so that we can describe our day-to-day life if our dream of having a baby came true. After talking to our families and some people we know who work and have families of their own, we confirmed that we wanted Early Childcare Education versus a nanny for the baby. Next, we explored our childcare options if we went back to our condo in the city once we had a baby, and surprisingly, we also looked into our options if we stayed living out here. My parents and Ryan's mom are willing to help support us if the baby is sick and has to stay home but do not want the responsibility of weekly care at this stage of their life, which we totally understand. Aunt Elsa is also willing to help too when she and Uncle Riyen aren't traveling.

Once they got back from Australia, though, they started to plan their next trip since they don't have a home here, tying them down yet. This time they are thinking about going to Europe since Uncle Riyen enjoyed this adventure of seeing new places almost as much as Aunt Elsa does. His job in computer programming allows him the flexibility to work remotely, plus he never really took time off before he met Elsa, so his company is being very cooperative. Aunt Elsa believed that this little stone house was what made her dream of finding love possible, but now life is even better since she has someone to share her other love of traveling and adventure with.

Sometimes when I question whether this house is really magic, I look at them and believe that all things are possible. I try not to re-read the list of people and their dreams too often so that I can stay focused on our tasks, but Ryan and I often read the envelopes for the first two steps as a reminder of why we are living here. I am still tempted to read the future envelopes, but I am learning patience through this adventure we are on together. Although this step took much longer than I expected, I have grown so much that I am not frustrated any longer with this process. Even the depth of love, trust, and communication with Ryan has expanded to a level I never knew was possible. I mean, Ryan and I talked and loved each other before, yet somehow compared to how we share our thoughts and wishes now, it seems superficial.

This little stone house has really become a home for us, and our vacation was such a beautiful time together that we are already planning a short, long weekend getaway in a few months. It feels so natural to work from home one day a week that I am easing into two days now to see if that still aligns with the needs of my job. I am able to focus and be more productive working from home than I would have thought, although there is not a baby or even a puppy to distract me. Not having to get ready and drive to and from work gives me extra time to make dinner, so we are eating out less and eating healthier. Ryan has cut back on working so much overtime so that we no longer fall exhausted into bed each night.

"Morning. What are you doing awake so early?" Ryan asks as he turns toward me in bed.

"Just thinking about these last few months and how grateful I am for this little stone house and for you," I add as I give him a kiss.

"It has been an amazing few months."

"Do you think we have figured out enough details that we could finish the description today?" I ask, wondering about the answer myself.

"I think so, but should we do two versions? One for moving back into the city and the other for staying here?"

"I was thinking that even though I love our condo in the city, it might be better to stay here, especially since we are getting a dog soon, too," I say, testing to see Ryan's response since I know how much he loves our condo.

"I was thinking the same thing because it turns out Sarah and her husband are looking for a place to buy now, and since they are already renting it, we could see if they want to buy it from us?"

"Wow, are you sure you won't miss living in the bustling city?"

"I am sure I will miss it, but don't you like living here if we have a dog and kids?" Ryan asks.

"Kids and a dog. We have come a long way, baby," I say with a laugh.

"We have, and I really love our life together. I thought it was great before, but now it's amazing."

"I agree. I guess we were happy when we didn't know what we were missing," I say as I cuddle into him.

"Speaking of what we are missing," Ryan jokes, "Are we going to look at the puppies your friend told you about today still?"

"Definitely, but since the sun is not even up yet, maybe we should try to fall back asleep?"

"Fine," Ryan says as he kisses me, and we close our eyes.

As the puppies run around barking at our feet, Sally keeps apologizing.

"I think they are more demanding for attention than most puppies since their momma died giving birth to them. We have tried to give them extra love and attention, but they miss their mom, I am sure."

"That's such a sad story. It was so nice of you to take them all," I say as a little black one lays on Ryan's foot.

"We have a lot of our own animals since my husband is a veterinarian, but when he told me what happened, that the owner couldn't bear to take care of them when her beloved dog died giving birth, of course, I agreed to take care of them. It's been a little crazy, but John and I always wanted a lot of kids and animals," Sally laughs.

"You have four kids, right?" I ask. Sally and I work for the same company, yet in different departments.

"Yes, we adopted Paul when he was a baby, but then we were foster parents to the other three before we adopted them. Those three have the same birth mother," she explains.

"Wow, I can't believe I didn't know that?"

"We don't shy away from talking about the adoptions, but they are my kids in my heart, and I am their mom, so it doesn't always come up."

"Ryan and I are trying to start a family, but it's not happening," I blurt out.

"Well, if you ever get to the point of thinking about adoption or fostering, let me know. It's been a wonderful experience for me, and like I said, these are my kids, and I couldn't love them anymore even if I gave birth to them."

"Thank you," I say, thinking about her words as I see Ryan looking down lovingly at the black ball of fur that seems to be somehow falling asleep on his foot.

"I think you have a fan," I say as Ryan bends down to pet her.

"She is the runt of the litter and almost didn't make it. She's a sweet one, though," Sally says, "I will be right back. I hear John calling me."

"She's so soft," Ryan says as we sit down on the grass, and she wakes up to crawl onto his lap.

"I think she picked you," I smile as I pet the other puppies.

"So, is Pepper our puppy?" I ask Ryan after the puppy sleeps on his lap for twenty minutes. The other ones head back to their beds to nap as if giving up all hope of being chosen.

"Who is Pepper?" Ryan says, looking up at me with a smirk.

"Our new dog," I laugh, "Pepper seems like a good name for her."

"I was thinking of the name Lucky?" Ryan says as a question.

"Why? Because she is so lucky to have you?" I say back with a chuckle.

"No, because we are so LUCKY to have her," he replies as she opens up her eyes as if saying yes, please.

"Let me go talk to Sally about the details of when we can take her home since she is so little," I say.

"Okay, I will be here with Lucky," he answers without looking up.

Sunday, June 7

After breakfast and a trip to the pet store to get all of the items we need to own a dog, we head out to spend time with Lucky again. Since she doesn't have a mom to nurse from, she is spending more time with Sally and John since they know how to take care of her properly. We still want to go see her, though, and assure Lucky that she is part of our family. If she keeps growing, they said we could take her home in a couple of weeks. Since I am working from home on Thursdays, I took off that Friday so that she can hopefully come home with us Wednesday evening, and we will be home all weekend with her.

"Since we finalized our two scenarios of life with a dog and then life with a baby, do we want to read the next step?" Ryan asks as we drive to see Lucky.

"I had thought the same thing but wondered if we needed to see what it is actually like with Lucky at home first?"

"We could re-read step two to be sure, but it seemed like we just needed to create a realistic description of what we think in truth, not what really happens," he says with a question.

"I think you are right. Maybe after visiting Lucky, we can get a bite to eat and go home and read envelope three," I suggest. I can't believe seven weeks have actually passed since we first read envelope two. I remember thinking that I could not make it even a week until the next step, but we took this step seriously, and it went by quickly.

"Sounds good. I wonder if Lucky misses us," he asks so sadly that I have to smile.

"I bet she does," I respond with my heart bursting with love for my husband.

Sunday Evening, June 7

"I think I need a glass of water before we open this envelope. Do you want one too?" I say, suddenly nervous. I have wanted to open this next envelope for weeks, but now that the moment is upon us, I am worried, wondering what our next task will be and how long it will take to complete.

"Yes, I feel nervous, too, wondering what we need to do next. That last one was pretty intense," Ryan mirrors my thoughts.

When I sit back at the kitchen table with our glasses of water, I see that Ryan got the book of dreams and the envelopes.

"I will re-read the last two envelopes, but it is your turn to read the third one, Tara, okay?"

After we read both envelopes and reflect on the tasks assigned to us these last few months, we decide to look at all of the dreams that have come true for others who have lived in this special house over the years before opening the third envelope. The first two envelopes have definitely brought us on a journey that we never expected.

- *Believing is a simple task that takes much effort.*
- *Examine your heart and your life to see what you really desire.*

"By the date of the first entry, it seems to have started in the 1920s, but do you ever wonder how and who discovered the magic of this house?" Ryan says as I look at the book.

"I never thought about it before, but you are right. I wonder how they did find out that it was magical," I reply, still distracted by the task of reading envelope three.

"Now the front of this envelope says, *'Gratitude is where life begins and ends.'* Are you ready, or do you want to wait a little longer?" Ryan asks.

I look around this little stone house that we have made into our home.

"Should we wait?" Ryan asks again.

"No, I am ready. I do believe in this house, and I think we really dug deep in step two," I reply as Ryan hands me the envelope. I open the clasp revealing yet another worn piece of paper to begin our third step.

Congratulations on completing the second step of this adventure. Your next step, step three, is to understand that life begins and ends in a state of gratitude. You cannot move to the next envelope, step four, until six weeks from today, so that it becomes second nature to you to live in this state of being thankful. Your task is simple, each day at the same time, either when you rise or go to sleep, you must name one thing that you are grateful for. They cannot be repeated, and it must be a complete thought, not just one word. You can do this any way you see fit, yet it should be fun and bring you joy. This little stone house contains the remarkable power to make your dreams come true, but in order to manifest your dreams, you will need to continue to believe, as well as take these necessary steps along the way. Remember also, as it will be with all steps, you cannot read ahead; each envelope must only be opened when the current exercise is completed, and you must not tell others what these envelopes say unless and until it is their turn to have their dreams come true.

After re-reading it again, I laugh, thinking this should be so easy. I don't like that we are required to stay on this step for six weeks, but I am learning that I need to be patient to understand and believe in the process. I already know that I am grateful for Ryan, our families, our health and careers, and especially for this little stone house.

"What are you laughing about?" Ryan asks.

"I was just thinking how easy this one should be. Don't you think?"

"I am not sure. We can't repeat anything, so that is forty-two things that we are each grateful for, and it can't just be a word. It needs to be specific, so I don't know," Ryan says cautiously.

"Hmm, well, how should we do this so that will be fun?"

"Let's look for ideas," Ryan offers as he pulls out his phone, "We could each do gratitude journals?"

"Any other ideas?" I ask as I get up and go sit on his lap to look at his phone.

"How about a gratitude tree with sticky notes?" he reads next.

"I don't know. Can we write full thoughts on a sticky note, and where would we post it?"

"True, and that would be forty-two or maybe even eighty-four sticky notes if we do ours separately? Let's see what else we can come up with."

"Okay," I agree, thinking that I wouldn't want that hanging somewhere for six weeks.

"Here's an idea. How about a gratitude jar?" Ryan says.

"I like that. Do we each have one jar or separate ones? When do we read them?" I ask, really liking this idea.

"Maybe each separate, and we wait to read them until the end so that we don't influence each other."

"It's too late to go shopping for one big jar or two little ones now. We could go Saturday morning before we go see Lucky and then start in the evening?" I offer.

"I think we should start sooner since we need to do it for six weeks, and I guess we need little pieces of paper also to write on."

"Who's the impatient one now?" I tease.

"Me," Ryan laughs, "Aren't you working from home Wednesday? Could you meet me for dinner, and then we could shop for a jar and paper?"

"Sure," I respond.

"This should be an interesting one then, don't you think?"

"I think so too. That last envelope ended up bringing wonderful changes that I never expected."

"True. Maybe we can go visit Lucky during that day, too, instead of just waiting for the weekend?" Ryan suggests.

"I can call and ask Sally tomorrow, but we might need to get off work a little earlier to drive there?"

"Let me know if Sally says we can come, and I will make it work. Then I can write that I am grateful for Lucky," he laughs.

"What specifically about Lucky, though?" I say as I get up and walk to the sink.

"Her black fur," he responds, even though he knows that I was just teasing.

"She will be here whining to go out sooner than you know," I say, ruffling his hair.

"Maybe a baby will be waking us up at night sooner than we think too," Ryan says, lost in his thought.

I almost respond that I hope, but instead, I say, "I believe."

"Ready for bed?"

I fall asleep, making a note in my head of all of the things I am grateful for today, and realize that I am truly thankful for this life Ryan and I are living together, even if we haven't been blessed with a baby yet. What an adventure this little stone house on the corner is taking us on.

Wednesday, June 10

Sally said we could visit Lucky in the evening, so once we finish a quick and early dinner out, we head to the store to find our jar. We decided that we should each do our own daily. We are not sure if we will read them each week or wait until the end of the six weeks. If we are putting them together, we need a pretty big jar, I think, as we walk into a little store in Walton.

"I knew they opened this store a few years ago, but I have never come in here before," I say to Ryan, as a man with black hair says welcome.

"If we can't find what we want here, there are some other stores on the way to see Lucky."

"True," I say as I spot some mugs and containers in the back.

I am looking at all the signs, mugs, and coasters with positive affirmations on them when Ryan walks over carrying a jar with the words "Love is…" on it.

"Where did you find that? It's perfect," I say.

"The owner, Joplin, just got it in today. When I explained what we were looking for, he went into the back and brought it right out."

"Wow, what a coincidence," I reply.

"Or maybe the universe wants to help us," Ryan says with not a hint of sarcasm in his voice. I realize that he has changed so much over these last couple of months. I know we both made changes at work, and obviously, the biggest change was moving, but I just didn't understand how stressed and busy we both were.

"Today, I am going to write that I am so grateful for you," I tell him as I reach over and hug him.

"Don't tell me what you are going to write yet; you might influence mine. We still need to figure out when to read them," he laughs as we walk to the register to pay.

"Is there anything else you are looking for?" asks Joplin as Ryan sets the jar down.

"We need little pieces of paper too?" Ryan says.

"How about these?" he says as he shows us little notebooks with the words 'I am grateful for...' on them.

"Those are perfect," I say with a laugh.

"I am glad that you found what you need," he adds as he rings our items up. If we weren't going to see Lucky, I realize that I love this little shop and could shop more. Maybe I will see if my mom or Aunt Elsa want to come back sometime.

"That was a really nice store," I say as I drive toward Sally's.

"It is. Joplin said that he opened it a year ago," Ryan responds.

"I didn't hear you two even talking that much," I say, also surprised because usually, Ryan isn't much of a talker when meeting strangers.

"You were lost in looking around and reading all those signs and things," Ryan says, "I know I usually don't talk to others when we are out, but I just felt so comfortable around him like I met him before."

"I am definitely going back there. Maybe I will ask my mom to go too."

"She would love that. We should shop in some of these small businesses more often."

"We should. Do you think Lucky will be sleepy since we are going later than we usually do?" I ask as we pull into the driveway.

"I hope not," replies Ryan, looking anxious.

Saturday, June 27

"Maybe we should read these tomorrow," I say as I put my slip of paper in our gratitude jar and try to push it in even though it is pretty full.

"It is getting full. We could put them in an envelope and wait to read all of them at the end like we planned?" Ryan suggests as he folds his paper in half, putting it in too.

"The jar sure looked big enough when we bought it. Obviously, we didn't realize how full this would get when we decided that, but just like the jar seemed serendipitous, maybe the jar being full means that we should read them?"

"If we are going to read them tomorrow anyway, let's just do it now?" Ryan says with a laugh.

"Okay," I say as I pick up the jar and bring it over to the bed. As I start to dump them out on the bed, I realize that I am really excited to read what Ryan and I both wrote. It has only been seventeen days, but I am struggling to remember what I even wrote each day.

"So, how do we do this?" Ryan says.

"I think we are overthinking it. Let's just each pick up one and read it aloud, but wait actually, first let's read the envelope so we see if we followed the directions," I say as I get the third envelope that says *'Gratitude is where life begins and ends'* out of the drawer.

I open it and read, *"Your task is simple; on each day at the same time, either when you rise or go to sleep, you must name one thing that you are grateful for. They cannot be repeated, and it must be a complete thought, not just one word. You can do this any way you see fit, yet it should be fun and bring you joy."*

"I think I wrote a different thing each day, but it was harder to remember than I thought it would be," Ryan laughs.

"I was just thinking the same thing. Even though I am excited to see what you wrote, I can't wait to read what I wrote some days too."

As we take turns reading whichever paper we pick up, we see that we both mentioned things about this house, our family, and, of course, things about Lucky with a few work items too, but one made me cry. Ryan wrote, "Today, as every day, I am grateful for Tara. Specifically, I am grateful for her loving heart that has made me a more loving person as well." I had written specific ones about Ryan too, but something in this one touched me so deeply. Growing up, my parents urged us to be kind and loving to others, but somewhere along the way, I got so focused on achievements and success that the desire to help and encourage others got lost.

His words made me realize that I need to find a way to do this again. I am happy that he sees my loving heart and that he believes I have made him more loving, but how can I give that to others? Would anyone at work think that about me? My family might say that I have a loving heart, and people at work hopefully see me as a kind person, but I have been so busy focusing on myself that I am not sharing that with others, encouraging or inspiring them.

I explain all of this to Ryan after we finish reading the rest and putting the papers in an envelope. I ask if I could keep this one out as a reminder of who I want to be.

"I love you, Tara. You might not think it, but you do inspire others to be kind just because you are such a loving person," Ryan says in my ear as we snuggle in bed.

"I love you so much, Ryan, and that is sweet of you to say, but I have just been so absorbed in work and in my sadness that we couldn't get pregnant that I think I lost sight of all the other people going through stuff and suffering, even suffering way worse things than me."

"I know; I realized as we read what we are grateful for, that we really are fortunate. We may not have a baby, but we have each other, wonderful families, jobs that pay well, and, of course, this great home and soon-to-be puppy," Ryan adds.

"Just doing this gratitude jar for two weeks has really helped me change the focus from what I don't have so that I can see all that I do have. Your words tonight really make me want to find a way to give back," I say.

"Well, just keep your eyes and ears open for something that speaks to you. We have almost four more weeks of writing these notes left, so who know what other surprises it will bring," Ryan says as he starts to fall asleep.

I am tired too, but I just keep thinking about how I can make a difference. I haven't volunteered anywhere since I was in college, so maybe I can do that. We should be bringing Lucky home this week, though, so I don't want something that takes me away from helping her feel safe and secure. I guess, like Ryan said, I could keep my eyes and ears open and see what comes to me.

A few months ago, I never imagined that he would be giving me that type of advice and that I would believe it could happen that way. The old Tara and Ryan would have thought about it and made a plan to make it happen, but actually, a couple of months ago, all I could think about was myself and what I needed and deserved. I know that I wrote that I was grateful for this house, but it is so much more than that. I am grateful for the changes in me that this house, our home, is helping me to make.

Wednesday, July 1

"So you will pick me up at work today at 5 pm sharp?" Ryan asks while drinking his coffee.

"For the tenth time, yes, I will," I laugh.

"I have only asked five times," he chuckles back.

"I can't believe Lucky is coming home with us tonight. Sally thinks she is ready, and with us both having off work for the long holiday weekend, we can help her feel safe and loved," I say as I get on my shoes to leave for work.

"What if she doesn't like it here?"

"Oh, Ryan, she will love being anywhere that you are. You know how sad she looks when we have to leave after visiting her," I say as I hug him goodbye, "Now let's go if you want a ride to the train today."

"I wish that I didn't have to work tomorrow."

"I know, but I will be here all day with her since I am working from home. I promise to take good care of her. I asked if I can work from home three days a week now just until she gets comfortable here too."

"I wish that I could work from home too," he says as we walk out the door and get in the car.

"Maybe you should look for a different job," I offer.

"It's a really good job, though."

"I was joking," I say as we pull out of the driveway, but now wondering if he should.

"Have you thought more about finding a way to give back?"

"Not yet, but I am keeping my ears open for opportunities. Right now, I just want to focus on making sure that Lucky feels loved."

"I can't believe that we are getting a dog," he squeals like a little kid, full of excitement.

Instead of teasing him, I just say, "We should have done this long ago."

Since I am working from home tomorrow and am taking a four-day weekend, I am swamped at work trying to get done so that I can pick up Ryan to drive out and get Lucky this evening. We have a little bed and a toy in the back in a cage for the ride home. I know Ryan would love to hold her on his lap, but since she hasn't been in a car since she was born, we thought this was best and also the safest for her.

I text Ryan as I get to the car that am leaving work now. He responds immediately, which is unlike him when he is working. I pull up in front of his building and see that he is already waiting. I so want to tease him, but my heart swells with love knowing that he has wanted a dog since he was a little boy.

"Ready to become a dog-dad?" I ask.

"I already am; we just need to bring her home."

"That is true," I say as we head for the expressway.

Sunday, July 5

The sun is barely up when I hear Lucky moving around in her cage to go out. We want to let her eventually sleep on her doggie bed, but until she is house-trained, we decided that she should sleep in her cage. She doesn't seem to mind it with a pad and some toys in there. We have been home with her since Wednesday, when we got her, and she has only had a couple of accidents. Obviously, it will be harder once we go back to work.

"Ryan, wake up. It's your turn to take her out," I say, since I took her out around midnight last night.

"Okay," he says as he crawls out of bed. She is a sweet little puppy and seems to have adjusted to living here already, but training her is a little harder than we both thought. I guess that I didn't realize she wouldn't be able to go all night without needing to go out. I roll over to my side to try and get a few more hours of sleep before she wakes up again.

I look at the clock and see that it is already almost nine, and wonder where Ryan and Lucky are. I smell coffee, so maybe Ryan stayed up after putting her out.

"Hi honey," I say walking into the kitchen where Ryan is reading the paper, and Lucky is sleeping at his feet.

"You stayed up?" I ask, as I pour a cup of coffee.

"Yes, I took her for a walk and decided to let you sleep."

"Want another cup?" I ask, as I add some milk to mine.

"No, I think that I have had three already," he laughs.

After reading the paper, we decide to take Lucky for another walk. Since it is getting hot out, we cut it short and ask Ryan's mom, Helene, if she wants to meet us for lunch. She lives about an hour from us and had invited us over for a barbecue yesterday, but since we just got Lucky, we didn't want to leave her alone all day long.

"Do you think Lucky will be okay?" Ryan asks as we drive to meet his mother.

"Yes, it can be a quick lunch; plus, since your mom is willing to meet us halfway between our homes, we won't be gone long," I reassure him. Ryan's mom lives a very busy life ever since his dad died suddenly of a heart attack during Ryan's senior year of college. At first, she was lost in her grief, but then she became active with the American Heart Association and helping others who have lost their loved ones. She is always busy working, volunteering, and going places with her large group of friends. At first, she was so overly protective and worried that something bad was going to happen to Ryan too, but she put in the work to learn how to handle her fears. I am sure that she still worries since he is her child, but she tries to keep her anxiety from interfering with their relationship.

We spend most of the meal looking at pictures of Lucky that Ryan has on his phone, but when we are leaving, his mom asks cautiously, "Any news on the baby front?"

Surprisingly, I don't cry or shut down like I did a few months ago, and I am able to say, "No, but we might try in-vitro, and we have even discussed becoming foster parents."

When Ryan suggested it after Sally telling us how they were foster parents, I wasn't open to it at all, but the more we talk about it, the more I think about all of the children who need love and a family.

"Really?" is all Helene says.

"We will let you know if we decide anything, Mom. Right now

though, Lucky is keeping us busy," Ryan responds as he gives her a hug goodbye.

After we drive away, I think about how little I really know about Ryan's mom. Ryan talks to her every week, but since we, including her, have been so busy with work and stuff, I never really think to call her. Ryan is an only child and says that he had a good childhood, but just that his parents were busy themselves with work and just expected him to excel and be successful, so he just pursued that. I am close with my mother, so she is who I turn to if I need advice or just to talk to.

"I wonder if your mom would like to go shopping with me sometime?" I say as we drive home.

"I am sure that she would like that," he says, "I probably should see her more often too, but she is always busy."

"Is she busy because we don't spend time with her, or do we not spend time with her because she is so busy?" I say more rhetorically.

"Hmm," Ryan responds, but then adds, "I wonder what Lucky is doing?"

She is sleeping peacefully in her cage when we get home.

After going out in her dog run and a quick game of fetch, Lucky falls asleep on the couch next to Ryan. I think of all the things that I could write on my gratitude paper today as I look at them and smile.

Sunday, July 12

Since our jar was bursting over again, we are sitting at the table to read what we are grateful for now. We tried to in the bedroom, but Lucky just kept jumping around. We could have put her in the cage, but since she is a big part of our life now, we just decided to move to the table to read them. I can't believe that a month has passed by so quickly, although Lucky is definitely keeping us busy. She rarely has an accident in the house anymore, but she has decided to chew anything we accidentally leave out.

There are no tears or surprises this time since most of Ryan's daily gratitude sentences focused on things Lucky did. I am working from home two days again this week, but we will be leaving her three days alone.

"Should we look into getting a dog walker, maybe?" I ask after we put these papers into another envelope.

"They have those?" Ryan asks.

"Yes," I chuckle at his question.

"I do feel bad that she is alone all day. How do you find a dog walker?"

"I can ask around at work tomorrow," I say.

"I was going to see if I could drive to work so that I could come to walk her part way through the day, but then I might have to work later to get everything done," he explains.

We put her in her cage when we both worked in the office, but she was out free the days I worked at home, and then Ryan ended up taking Friday off last week, so she had us both home.

"She did seem fine on her own, but that was only one day," I say, the add, "Let me see if my mom or dad are free tomorrow to let her out part way through the day. I know they can't every day, so let's see if we can hire someone. I am getting used to having you home at a decent time for dinner."

"I agree that I don't want to start working so late again."

"I might go to that shop in town today where we got the gratitude jar, so I can see if my mom wants to go and ask her then?"

"Okay. I can also ask my mom too for this week, but I am not sure if she can," Ryan offers. I still haven't reached out to his mom to meet for lunch, but I am planning on it.

Later as my mom, Aunt Elsa, and I walk through downtown, I wonder why we don't do this more often. They both said they could help with putting Lucky out until we can hire a dog walker. Ryan's mom is traveling, but she told him that she could do it next week, if we still need her.

"This is the store we got the gratitude jar in," I say as we approach the door. Aunt Elsa loved how we decided to do this step. My mom just thought we came up with the idea on our own since we can't tell her about the envelopes or the steps. She knows that Aunt Elsa thinks the house is special and wanted us to move there, but it is hard that we are not able to share all of the secrets of this little stone house with her.

"Hello, Elsa. Hi Sophia," says Joplin when we enter the store.

"Hi, Joplin," says my mother as she goes over to give him a hug. I should have known that she already knew about this place.

"I guess that I am the only one who didn't know about this place," I laugh.

"I should have guessed that you were related when you and your husband bought that jar a few weeks ago. How do you like it?" Joplin asks.

"It is perfect," I reply as I start looking around as Elsa and my mom chat with Joplin.

After they tell him about our new puppy, he shows me a dog walker sign on the community corkboard.

"Do you know her?" I ask as I take a picture of the card and send a quick text to the number on it.

"Nicky is a guy, and I just met him when he put the card there. He seemed nice; he said that she just moved to the area. He was young and sort of quiet," he explains.

We are about to leave when I see a set of paints and a blank canvas. I remember when I was in high school, and would take art classes. I don't know why I never took any in college, but something urges me to buy them.

"Are you painting again?" my mom asks as if painting was something I did all of the time and not something I haven't done since high school.

"It is funny but now that Ryan has a dog, I seem to have more free time on the weekend. Maybe I will give it a try again."

"I think I have that painting you did back in high school still," my mother says.

"Really? Do you remember what it was of?" I ask, trying to remember.

"I think it was a flower, maybe?" she says.

"A red rose," I reply, as I remember.

"Yes, that was it," she says, as I wonder why I didn't keep painting.

Saturday, July 25

Even though Tuesday was the last day of our six weeks of doing the gratitude exercise, we decided to wait until today to read the next envelope. As we read the last of our papers and reflected on doing this, we both decided that we want to still add slips to the jar when we feel the urge to and check the jar monthly. We also said that if either of us starts focusing on what we don't have again instead of all that we do have, we should call each other out on it and revisit this exercise.

"Before we read the next envelope, I have a gift for you," Ryan says as he hands me a blue gift bag, my mind racing, trying to figure out if I missed our anniversary or a birthday.

"What is this for?" I ask as I open the bag. In it, I find a small frame with the paper that Ryan wrote saying, "*Today, as every day, I am grateful for Tara. Specifically, I am grateful for her loving heart that has made me a more loving person, as well.*"

"I don't want you to every forget how special you are to me. I know you haven't found your way to show that kindness and love to others yet, but I want you to always know how much you mean to me," he says and then adds with a chuckle, "and to Lucky now."

"Thank you, Ryan. I love you," I say with a tear in my eye.

"Do you think you could find a way to help others through painting? You are really good. I can't believe you kept this talent from me for all these years."

"Thank you, but I think painting is just for me, but I am keeping my ears and eyes open to find a way to help others. I have had a couple of ideas, but none of them felt right."

"Well, you will find something. I am glad that you reconnected with painting. Are we ready to move to step four?"

"Me too, and yes, I think that we are," I answer as I get up to get the book and the other envelopes.

I have learned that as I focus more and more on what I have in my life to be grateful for and less on what I am lacking, the list of items to be thankful for seems to just grow and expand.

"**Intentions** create reality."

Sunday, July 26

Yesterday after reading the past three envelopes and looking through the book of dreams, Ryan opened the fourth envelope with the words. *Intentions create reality* on the top and read the following words.

Congratulations on completing the third step of this adventure. After six weeks of living in a place of daily gratitude, you should be feeling much lighter. Your next step, step four, is to understand that intentions create reality. Although that may sound like a simple truth, it is much more complex than it appears because often people are not aware of their intentions. Also, we shouldn't take anything personally since we create collectively, as well as individually. Remember that you can't control everything that happens in life. Not everything happens for a reason; some things are just random events in a multi-creating universe. Although we can and do create individually, group intentions also assist as well as interfere with your individual ones. You cannot move to the next envelope, step five, until you complete the following items. There are four questions to answer, but you can only do one a day. Then there are also three tasks to complete. You can take longer than seven days but not less than. This little stone house contains the remarkable power to make your dreams come true, but in order to manifest your dreams, you will need to continue to believe, as well as take these necessary steps along the way. Remember also, as it will be with all steps, you cannot read ahead; each envelope must only be opened when the current exercise is completed, and you must not tell others what these envelopes say unless and until it is their turn to have their dreams come true.

I spent all day yesterday re-reading the fourth envelope. Ryan said that I am overthinking it, but I just keep wondering that if our intentions really do create our reality, what were my intentions all these years? Wasn't my intention these last few years to get pregnant and become a mother? Why didn't it happen then, and how can I make it happen now? What intentions influence my intention of becoming a mother? Is it only Ryan and I, or do my parents influence it? I am not sure why this step is bothering me so much. We decided yesterday that we would start fresh today since there is a task or question for each of the next seven days. I am excited that this step will not last six weeks, but I already can tell that this will not be an easy one for me.

"Ready to read the first task?" Ryan asks cheerfully when I walk into the kitchen.

"How can you be so happy about this? If our intentions create, then why can't we have a baby? Isn't getting pregnant and starting a family what we both want?" I ask for the fifth time.

"Tara, honey. You know it is not that simple. Let's see what we need to do today, and then we can discuss it more."

"Fine, where is the card for today?" I say as I notice the envelope on the table in front of him.

He hands me the card with the number one on it, and I begin to read, still standing, *"Refer back to your exercise in step two. Examine your heart and life to determine your true desires. What were the three things that you would make come true if you could, and reflect on what actions you took to reach them? Did you remember them as you completed the six weeks of gratitude exercise, and are you still making steps towards them?"*

"So mine were a vacation, a dog and a baby, so I would say that I am doing pretty well," Ryan says immediately.

"How can you say that? We still don't have a baby?" I ask.

"I know, but at least we have two of them now. That is more than we had when we moved to this house and started this process."

"I guess, but we haven't taken any steps toward having a baby," I say.

"Well, let's both reflect on that one and come up with some steps we could take."

"Okay," I agree, realizing that Ryan is really growing and changing from doing these things. Maybe he was a deep thinker all along, but he didn't share that part of himself with me as much.

"I can think of one thing we could do to work on it," he says with a grin as he grabs me and gives me a kiss, and I kiss him back.

Wednesday, July 29

We decided that we are going to talk to the fertility specialist about our options, and I also called Sally to get information about adopting or maybe becoming foster parents. We are not sure where either of these two actions will lead us, but if intentions can create, then we want to make sure that the universe knows that we are serious about adding to our family. We have only had Lucky for a short time, and Ryan was the one who wanted a dog, but now I can't even imagine our life without her. The next cards that we read Monday and Tuesday definitely challenged Ryan and I both.

We read them before work so that we could journal and reflect on our answers separately, but then we had deep and true discussions both nights after work about our answers. Card #2 was *"When do you feel alive and time just flies by? What makes you feel happy, and what makes you feel at peace? When are you most joyful?"* Being with Lucky was Ryan's answer, and mine was painting. Our answers surprised us both since neither of these were part of our life until recently.

Tuesday's card #3 was interesting to contemplate asking us, *"What are you fighting or resisting? Are you spending more time fighting what you don't want in your life? Because, remember, that what you resist will persist because you are creating that by focusing on it."* I realized that I have been focusing more on not getting pregnant, so was that contributing to why I can't get pregnant? I know that it is complicated, and some people have physical reasons they can't get pregnant, but I might have a beginning understanding of this idea of intentions creating.

Before Ryan left for work today, we read card #4, that was based on envelope two also, *"Review your description of what your day-to-day life would look like if this dream came true and adjust it, if necessary, based on your answers to cards 1-3 and your gratitude practice that you did for the six weeks."*

Since I am working from home today, I can't stop thinking about how different my life is right now from what I even imagined it would look like. After a short walk with Lucky and a quick sandwich for lunch, I am writing out a description of my day-to-day life right now and trying to figure out how it would look if I had a baby right now.

Would I still be working? Would I need our dog walker, Nicky, to come walk Lucky more often, or could I do that with a baby?

I realize that I don't know much about Nicky except that he just moved in with his mother and is new to the area. He was able to provide some references, and Lucky seemed to like him right away.

We had him start on the weekend and some of the days that I worked from home to see how it went. Lucky didn't even resist; she went with him easily and was still happy yet tired after her walk. He is very polite but very quiet. Maybe I could see if he wants to have coffee or tea sometime just to get to know him better.

Since I don't have a commute, I decide to get a little painting done after work before Ryan gets home.

"Hi, Tara. Well, hello, Lucky," said Ryan as he walks in the door.

"I didn't realize it was that late," I reply as I look up from my painting.

"Wow, your painting is really coming along."

"I thought I would spend just a little time on the background before starting dinner. I don't know where the time went. I can order something instead of cooking if you are really hungry."

I guess I do get lost in painting.

"Why don't we just order pizza so we can talk about card #4," Ryan suggests as he undoes his tie, "I can take Lucky for a quick walk while you paint."

"Okay, I need to let the paint dry anyway so I can clean up and order the pizza. Are you in the mood for deep dish or thin?" I ask as I watch him sit on the floor in his suit, grinning from ear to ear.

"Either is fine," Ryan says as he scratches Lucky behind her ear, "How's my girl today?"

Friday, July 31

Since Ryan was going to be in court all day Thursday, we agreed to wait until today to do card #5 or task #1. When we read it at breakfast yesterday, and it said, *"Today is a day of contemplation,"* he looked at me with a look of shock. We knew that he couldn't commit to it, and I knew that it would be challenging for me at the office as well. Ryan is just working in his office, and since I am working from home today, we knew that it would be easier for both of us to do it today. It was tough even to do this morning, but we got up earlier than usual, and we re-read the card again before doing it this morning.

It said that we must *"Spend ten minutes in quiet meditation at least five times over the course of the day releasing negative feelings out and positive feelings in with our deep breaths, inhaling in with the good, out with the bad. If you are not able to do all five times, you must wait until a day when you are able. You can do this out in nature or in your home. You can close your eyes or use an item like a candle to stare at it. The purpose is to clear your mind of all thoughts and see what comes into your consciousness, to see the truth of self."* It also said, *"Sometimes it is helpful to repeat a word or sound."*

I have never really meditated before, so I might try different ways each time. We didn't talk about it when we tried it together before work, but I know that it was hard for me to sit quietly for ten minutes. I just kept thinking about Lucky, wondering where she went, and thinking about how many more minutes that I had to do this. It was difficult not to look over at Ryan since we agreed to do it together with our eyes closed.

When the alarm went off, we just kissed, and off Ryan went to catch his train. Hopefully Ryan can do it twice at work today, or we might need to stay at this card again tomorrow. Nothing really came into my thoughts that had any real meaning. Maybe this activity won't hold much meaning or impact.

I work for a couple of hours, but after taking Lucky on a quick walk, I decide to sit outside to do my next ten minutes of silence before it gets too hot. I keep my eyes open and focus, or should I say try to un-focus, as I look at a flower I cut from our garden. Once again, nothing really comes into my consciousness, but I feel very peaceful and relaxed after these ten minutes. I even thought about doing it longer but decided to get back to work before eating lunch and walking Lucky again.

After a few more hours of work, I decide to stay inside and sit in the kitchen this time. Since I am feeling so positive, I focus on the word peace, repeating it over and over as I keep my eyes closed. I am surprised when my alarm goes off after ten minutes. Surprisingly, I really feel calm, although once again, no big revelation came into my thoughts. I might continue this daily, although not five times a day after we finish this step.

I send a quick text to Ryan asking how his day is going. He just texted, "Okay. Hope your day is good."

I really want to ask if he has done it twice at work, but I know that we each are committed to the process and the steps laid out in the envelopes.

The rest of the afternoon flies by after I take Lucky out again. I am feeling very focused and productive and am almost done working for the day when I hear the door open.

"Hello, Lucky," I hear Ryan as she goes running to him.

"You are home early," I say as I walk to the door.

"Yeah, can we talk about it once you are done working? I know it's still early, and you have work to do today," Ryan says solemnly.

"I actually think that I am almost done. I was very productive this afternoon. I think the meditating did help me focus more," I explain and then ask, "How did yours go?"

"Can we talk about it once you finish working? I want to go get changed and walk Lucky."

"Okay," I agree, but wanting to really ask more.

I finish up my work while Ryan showers and plays with Lucky. I was going to ask if he is sick since he left work early, which he never does, but he seems okay except maybe quiet. I get us both a glass of water and head into the bedroom, where Lucky and Ryan are lying on the bed watching TV.

"I am done working. Here's a glass of water," I say.

"Thanks," he says, taking a drink and then turning off the TV.

"Tara, I am sorry, but I don't think I can do this?" Ryan says without making eye contact.

"What do you mean?" I ask, completely lost.

"I can't do the meditating or quiet contemplation step."

I am not sure what to ask or even how to respond, so I just sit and take his hand. I realize that he is shaking as he begins to explain.

"I don't know Tara, this morning was fine except that I had trouble focusing. Then when I took a break from work to do it in the morning, something just stirred in me, but I didn't really know what. I was hesitant to do it again in the afternoon, but I decided that I was being silly since I wasn't even sure what I was feeling."

He pauses, and Lucky instinctively snuggles up close to him. I, too, lay down, and he holds me tight while he tries to continue.

"I don't know why, but all I could see was my father in his coffin from his funeral. I didn't even cry then, but here I was, sobbing on the deck outside of work. Luckily no one was there, but I just couldn't keep my eyes closed. I don't know what it meant, but I just don't think I can go there again."

After a few minutes of just holding him, I say quietly, "It is up to you, Ryan. I support whatever decision you make. You obviously know how much I want a baby, but I want you more that anything else. Because I love you so much, I do need to say that maybe you need to explore what you experienced to understand what it means, though, honey."

"I know, but I just don't know if I can."

"Let's just lay here together, and you can absorb the love that Lucky and I are sending to you, okay?"

"Okay, but I am not meditating," he laughs sadly.

"I love you," I say as Lucky licks his arm as if saying I love you too.

I am not sure how long we lay like this, dozing off and on, but we finally get up to make dinner without mentioning the fact that we are expected to meditate two more times today.

After we make chicken and pasta with a salad for dinner, Ryan blurts out, "Fine, let's try it together again."

I explain how I sat outside looking at the cut flower when I did it this morning, so we head outside. Lucky runs around for a minute but then settles at our feet. I want to ask Ryan if he is sure, but I can see that he is trying to be brave. We both look at the flower, and I repeat the word peace in my head again because I want to distract myself from staring at Ryan. This time when I do it, I feel such an enormous amount of love for my husband. I know in my head that we are already a family, but I have been denying that fact with my desire to have a baby. When the alarm goes off, I reach over and see that he has tears on his face, but he has a look of contentedness too.

"You okay, baby?" I ask as Lucky once again licks him.

"Yes, I saw my father dead again, but I also was able to remember him alive. I am still not sure what it all means, but I am glad that we did this."

"Me too. I realized that in my heart, I know that we are a family already. I still want a baby, don't get me wrong, but we are enough. You are enough and always have been. I hope I never made you feel like you weren't."

"I always knew that you loved me, but I felt like I was constantly disappointing you because you weren't getting pregnant," he answers.

"I am truly sorry, Ryan. I never blamed you, and I am sorry if I made you think I did. If anything, I felt like the failure," I explain.

"You are never a failure, no matter what happens with having a baby. I love our life together, Tara."

"I do too, Ryan," I say with a tear in my eye as we hug.

"Let's go walk our current baby, Lucky," Ryan laughs as Lucky jumps up.

"Okay," I laugh.

Before bed, we decide to do our last meditation together with our eyes closed. I tell him about repeating the word peace as another way to do it.

Ryan was quiet once we were done, but as we drift off to sleep, he says quietly, "I realize that I have a deep fear of dying and leaving you and our child alone because of my father's death. I guess the fear was always there, but until I sat alone with my thoughts through this exercise, I wouldn't acknowledge it. As if that somehow made it not real."

"That had to be hard losing your dad so young and so suddenly. You know that there is no guarantees in life, but it probably won't happen to you."

"I know rationally, but I am afraid. What I realized is that if it were going to happen, it would happen even if I never had a baby. I know that if we had a child and I died, you would be a great mom on your own, but I don't want a child to feel what I feel," Ryan explains.

"And I know if anything happened to me, you would be a great dad on your own."

"Let's just make sure we both live long lives," Ryan chuckles nervously, trying to make light of his fears.

"Okay."

"You never said how this last meditation went for you. Anything come up?"

"Just earlier about how we are already a family, but I really think my brain enjoys the quiet. I think I will keep doing it, but only once a day, maybe."

"Hmm, maybe I will try to keep it up too. Good night Tara."

I respond, "Night, I love you, Ryan," as I drift off to sleep, thinking that I need to tell him tomorrow that maybe he should see a counselor to help explore those feelings.

Sunday, August 2

I wake up thinking of certain words and items that I want on my vision board. In addition to gratitude, I want the word abundance. I may not have a baby, but I have an abundance of love and opportunities in my life. I jot them down before I even get out of bed. Ryan is still sleeping, so I get up to take Lucky out, make coffee, and meditate.

When we looked at our next task in this envelope, on card #6, our #2 task, it stated that we need to create a vision board. Yesterday, I went to the store to buy some magazines, poster boards, and markers. It explained that we could use pictures or drawings or simply write words or sentences. It must be clear what we intend to create or manifest in our lives. The tricky part is that we can have expectations, but it is important to let go of how we achieve the outcome.

When Ryan and I talked about it, we could see that someone dreaming about having money could surrender how the money comes to them, but us having a baby is harder to let go of. I never saw getting a dog as starting a family, and now I do, so I suppose my dream should be to expand our little family; however, the universe wants to.

It also said to NOT create the vision board until we are certain of our intentions, not an outcome. I know that I can have some expectations, but it is difficult to release the exact outcome or expectation of how it should manifest. The instructions were quite clear, though, that this is not a dream board.

It said to be careful because wanting to have patience may give us situations that we must be patient. Wanting to become more loving may cause us to encounter people who are difficult to love. We must be clear about what we are focusing on since whatever we focus on could increase. I worry that wanting a baby may create more feelings of "wanting a baby," not actually having one.

I remember a book I read in college that was similar to this. It explained that you should not put your problems at the center of your day because focusing on a problem will expand it. It's important to start each day instead by reflecting on what is right. On the worst day, there is always some good, so we should see that. I know these aren't new concepts, but it is a different way to look at life than I am used to.

When Ryan wakes up, he sees me at the kitchen table, flipping through the stack of magazines again, with Lucky at my feet.

"Good morning. Did you buy every magazine the store had?" Ryan laughs.

"No," I laugh, "But I figured looking through these could help us see what we are focusing on before we start on our boards."

"I am just teasing, but I do have a question. Do you think it's just our intentions for right now? I mean, there are so many things I would like to manifest in my life, but over time."

"The instructions didn't say, but my thought is that we focus on our immediate future. I am sure as time goes on, we can change these or make new ones," I say.

"I wonder if Elsa still has hers?" Ryan asks.

"Oh, you are right. We should ask her. Ready to get started, or do we need more time to be clear about our intentions?"

"I think we can start and just think as we choose words and images for our vision boards."

Monday, August 3

As I open my eyes this morning, I get the feeling that I am creating the life I always wanted but never knew or even believed was possible.

Before this adventure of the little stone house on the corner started, I guess I just thought that life had happened. Sure, we made choices, but I believed that we had less control over the outcome.

We decided to keep our vision boards in the bedroom so they are the first things we see each day when we wake up. They definitely took us a lot longer to make than we thought. Ryan found many pictures for on his, but I ended up drawing some pictures and writing in words to complete mine. Since we didn't finish them until late yesterday, we decided to get up a little early to read card #7. Ryan is taking Lucky out when I get out of the shower, so I get ready and am making coffee when he comes into the kitchen.

"So, card #7?"

"Let's see what surprise this one has for us," I laugh and hand Ryan this one to read.

"Okay, card #7 is an intention exercise. *Now that you completed your vision board and are keenly aware of what you are focusing on, you will focus on the power of "I am" statements,*" Ryan reads.

"Interesting," I say.

"There's more."

The card explained that all day or as long as it takes, we need to ponder the connection between behaviors and consequences. If I act happy, what is the consequence? If I respond in angry, what is the consequence? Once we feel confident in this connection between what we are being and the consequences, our task is to write out an "I am" statement. I am a mother is my dream, but can I write that as my statement?

"Is Nicky coming today to put Lucky out?" Ryan asks.

"Yep, he usually comes around noon to walk her and make sure she has water and treats," I say, even though he knows this already.

"Okay."

"Do you think this card will take longer than today?" I say the unspoken words between us.

"I think so. I can't even think of an "I am" statement to write," he explains.

"I feel the same way. Why don't we just do it all week and plan on writing our I am statements this weekend?" I offer.

"I wanted to suggest that, but I know how anxious you are to move onto each envelope, and I didn't want to delay it more," Ryan responds.

"I am trying to see this process as part of the journey now. In so many ways, I am learning more about myself, about you, and about us as a couple, and that wasn't even my dream," I explain.

"I feel the same way."

"Plus, I have someone's birthday to plan that is coming up on Saturday," I tease.

"Who has a birthday coming up?" Ryan jokes.

"I wonder," I laugh, giving him a hug, "I can't believe that my brother is even coming to town for it. Plus Riyen and Elsa, your mom, and my parents. Do you think we should invite some friends over, too, or just keep it family?"

"Since we rarely see your brother, let's keep it small so we can all talk more. Maybe we can do a separate party later in the month with friends to celebrate both of our birthdays since yours is coming up in September?" Ryan says.

"That's a good idea. I love our home, but this house is small if we wanted a lot of people here," I add.

"Although I am not sure what friends we would include anyway," Ryan says.

"True, it has been awhile since we went out with any friends."

"I might need help with this task. So what would our "I am" statement be now? What are we being so that we can see the consequence?" Ryan asks with a concerned look on his face.

"I don't know. I think we are being caring to think about my brother coming and wanting to spend time with him. Maybe this is going to be more difficult than we imagine," I laugh as I give him a hug.

"I agree."

"I love you. See, I am being loving to you now," I say with a laugh.

"That you are. I love you too," I hear him say as he puts the leash on Lucky to walk her once more before he catches his train to work.

Thursday, August 6

Even though it is August, the evening has a cool breeze as we sit outside eating dinner.

"So what do I do after I write my I am statement?" Ryan asks.

"It says on the next line, write it out again, but eliminate the last letter, then continue to write it out on the next line while eliminating another letter and so on until you have one letter left," I read to him. We were both able to think of our "I am" statements. After the initial challenge of connecting our behaviors to what we were being to see the consequences, we both seemed to grasp this concept, so we decided to do this last task earlier than planned. We also took tomorrow off work for Ryan's birthday, so we wanted to open the fifth envelope in the morning.

Once we finish writing our statements, the instructions said to hold this paper in our hand and surrender our I am statement to the universe, and then burn it in a safe spot, watching the embers and smoke, with our statement being released above. My statement was that, I am a caring, compassionate, hard-working, and giving person who loves my family. Ryan's was similar. We both tried to not focus on what we are not or what we want.

"I am going to meditate while it burns. Do you want to also?" I ask Ryan.

"Sure, I haven't really done it much. Are you doing it every day?"

"Sometimes, I even do it twice a day, when I work from home. I am surprised how much easier it is getting to clear my mind and just focus on an object like this fire or repeat a word. I really enjoy doing it as well."

"That's good. Let me try to do it, and see how I feel."

My alarm goes off once the ten minutes are up, so I ask Ryan, who is still quiet, "How did it go?"

"Good, nothing really came up like before, but I feel calm."

"Yeah, I usually feel refreshed. I enjoyed watching our statements burn and disappear into the universe," I explain as I touch the piece of burnt paper with a stick as the ashes collapse and become one with the fire.

"I can't believe that we are on envelope five. I wish we could open it now instead of in the morning," Ryan says after putting the fire out.

"We could. Nothing in the book or on the envelopes says we have to wait. I think we just got into the habit of opening in the mornings on the weekends."

"What do you think?"

"It's still early, and we don't work tomorrow. Let's read the other envelopes and look at the book of dreams that came true, and then see how we feel," I suggest.

"We better take Lucky for a walk first," Ryan says as she jumps on us, as we walk in the back door.

"She's mad we didn't let her come outside with us," I say.

"We had a fire burning, Lucky," Ryan says to her as he pets her belly.

"Conor was surprised when I told him that we got a dog," I say.

"Why? Does he think he is the only one who loves animals?" Ryan laughs.

My brother is almost six years younger than me, but when he left for college, he never came back really. He travels the world like my Aunt Elsa, but instead of writing about what he sees, he takes pictures. I think that he is an amazing photographer, and he does okay. However, he hasn't really had any great success with selling pictures to social media sites or traditional magazines. I know that my parents wish he would come home and get a regular job and a wife and kids, but I can't imagine Conor doing that.

"What do you mean?" I ask.

"He takes a lot of pictures of animals, doesn't he?"

"I don't know. I never really thought about it. He just takes a lot of pictures to me."

"Well, you should notice. He definitely takes a lot of animal pictures. Maybe he can take some of our Lucky," Ryan says.

"Because you don't take enough?" I tease.

"Funny. We better get going for our walk, though, or we'll be too tired to read the envelopes."

After a short walk, we sit on our bed to read through all four envelopes. We also spend time talking about and reflecting back on what we had to do for each, remembering each step. We realized that each envelope had so much meaning and brought such different things out in us and in our relationship. *Believing is a simple task; examine your heart and your life; gratitude is where life begins and ends, and intentions create reality.*

"This envelope says, '*Now is the moment.*' Do we want to read it tonight or wait until tomorrow?" Ryan asks.

"I think we should wait until morning," I say, "But we could tonight if you still want to?"

"No, let's wait until morning. I have so much to think about just reflecting back on this journey so far."

"Me too; I can't believe how much our life has changed in these four months."

"I am shocked how much I have changed even," Ryan adds.

"It is hard to imagine a life without Lucky," I say as we fall asleep, both thinking about our new life in this little stone house on the corner.

> *"**Now** is the moment. Live in this truth,*
> *not in the past or in the future."*

Friday, August 7

"I think that I need to write down exactly what I need to do. This step is a little confusing to me," I say to Ryan as we walk Lucky in the morning.

"I know what you mean. I am still thinking about the first task. It may take longer than one day to do it, especially with the party tomorrow."

"Let's give ourselves the weekend to do it and maybe start Monday with the second task of finding the 'gift' of now in each day?" I offer.

"Okay," Ryan agrees.

"I am going to re-read envelope five when we get back and take some notes."

I hold envelope five with the words *"Now is the moment"* in my hand, thinking about what those words mean before I open it. I read the words inside, jotting notes in my notebook.

Congratulations on completing the fourth step of this adventure. Your next step, step five, is "Now is the moment. Live in this truth, not in the past or in the future." Start this step by imagining yourself at each age and the events that passed or that will happen (5, 10, 15, 20, 30, 40, 50, 60, 70, 80, and so on). Reflect on what you were or will be doing, thinking, and feeling at that age and time. Once this task is complete, think about putting everything, good and bad, that you experienced in the past in your right hand; then, imagine all of your dreams and plans that you have for your future in your left hand. Now hold both hands in front of you; feel how heavy your hands are becoming holding the burden of the past and future in today. Once you can no longer hold the weight of your hands, clasp them together to live in the 'Now.'

For the next month, you must look for the "gift" of today, of the now. You must understand that you deserve joy and happiness today. This is more than gratitude; instead, you need to see the miracle of life that each day presents to you and take action where appropriate. Please repeat the hand visualization activity if you struggle to stay in the present, or you can create your own ritual to help you. You cannot open the last envelope, the final step, until you live in the now and stop focusing on the past and/or quit believing that you will only be happy once you have exactly what you want. This little stone house contains the remarkable power to make your dreams come true, but in order to manifest your dreams, you will need to continue to believe, as well as, take these necessary steps along the way. Remember also, as it will be with all steps, you cannot read ahead; each envelope must only be opened when the current exercise is completed, and you must not tell others what these envelopes say unless and until it is their turn to have their dreams come true.

I know that we have shopping to do for the party tomorrow and that my brother's flight will be in the late afternoon, but I decide to meditate before I start on this task of reflection. It gets a little easier each day to clear my mind and just be in the moment. Maybe that is what this step is all about, really learning to let everything go to stay in the present.

"Are you almost ready?" Ryan asks as I am finishing my hair.

"Almost," I reply, knowing that we should be leaving now to get to the airport on time to pick up Conor.

After meditating, we ran our errands, getting the rest of the food and drinks for Ryan's birthday party. We already had someone come clean the house and do the yard, so other than a few last-minute things and cooking tomorrow, I think we are ready.

"Do you think we should ask Nicky if he could come to walk Lucky tomorrow since we will be busy with the party?" Ryan asks as we head to the airport.

"Maybe that's a good idea. Let me text him and see if he is available tomorrow," I reply as I get my phone out, "I know we weren't inviting friends, but we could also ask him if he wants to stay for a little bit?"

"Sure. Are your parents meeting us for dinner once we get Conor today?" Ryan asks.

"That's the plan. I am not sure if Conor is staying with us or with our parents tonight. He said he didn't want to intrude since we have the party tomorrow."

"He definitely wouldn't be intruding since we are all ready for tomorrow, and I know you would love to spend time with him."

"I do, but so do Mom and Dad. He is home all week, but I know it will fly by."

"Yeah, and I guess he will stay tomorrow since your parents will want to head home earlier than him," Ryan says.

"Are you implying that my parents won't stay late and have bottles of wine with us?" I laugh as my phone chimes.

"Nicky can come tomorrow. Should I say around three and tell him he could stay for some food?"

"Definitely. Should we have asked him for tonight too?"

"No, I think Lucky should be fine until we get home. I don't think dinner will take long."

We are close to the airport when Conor texts that he landed and will be right out after he gets his bags. The airport is packed, but luckily we see Conor right away when we get to his terminal entrance. The car is barely stopped when I jump out to hug my little brother, who is actually almost half a foot taller than me.

He looks the same as when I saw him last, which was almost two years ago now. His hair is lighter than mine, but we still look alike with our brown hair and eyes. We both have wavy hair, but he keeps his short, and most of the time, I used to straighten mine. I am learning to love my curls now, though.

"Tara, be careful. You are going to get hit by a car," Conor exclaims as I hug him.

"I have missed you, Conor. Don't stay away this long again."

"You could come to visit me if you didn't work so much, you know?" he says as Ryan opens the back and shakes hands. They put his bags in, and then we all climb back in.

"Where's Lucky?" Conor asks, and I notice he has a camera in his hand.

"Ryan is right! You do love animals and take a lot of pictures of them."

"Not very observant, Sis, if you are just noticing that now when your husband tells you," he laughs.

"She looks at all of the pictures you take, Conor, but I can't believe she never noticed the slant toward animal pictures," Ryan joins in, laughing.

"We never had pets growing up. How was I to know you loved them?" I say.

"Mom and Dad wouldn't let us get any, that's why," he responds.

"I had no idea you wanted any, just like Ryan did."

"That's because all you did was study growing up. While I was outside looking for animals and adventure, you were at the library or learning about something."

"Well, not anymore. I, actually both of us, have cut back on working. We moved to the suburbs, got a dog, and even went on vacation."

"I couldn't believe that when you told me that the first time. I really thought you were playing a prank on me. But in all seriousness, you look different. I don't know; somehow, you seem healthier and more free. These changes look good on you. On you too, Ryan," Conor says as he touches Ryan on the shoulder from the back seat.

"Thank you, we were happy before but even more now," Ryan says.

"I can't wait to hear more about you and what's going on," I say. Even though I want to ask if he is dating anyone, I know from everyone asking me about having a baby that it hurts when you want something that isn't happening, and people constantly ask.

"There's not much to tell, but we can talk at dinner. Are Mom and Dad on their way?"

"Yes, they are already at the restaurant, even though we told them that we wouldn't be there until closer to six," I explain.

"Did you just take a picture of me, I ask," when I hear the click of Conor's camera.

"Yep, you know me. I can't resist a good animal picture," he teases.

"Nice," I laugh.

After dinner, catching up, and lots of laughter, Ryan, Conor, and I head home. Since he will stay with our parents during the week while we work, Conor offered to help us prepare for the party. I didn't tell him that there isn't much to do since I am eager to spend as much time with him as I can.

I have always loved Conor and felt close to him, but as he said, we really were two different people growing up with such separate interests. I feel like I have changed so much just in these few months that maybe we can find more common ground and grow even closer.

As Ryan suspected, Lucky immediately fell in love with Conor and won't stop following him once we got home, which was fine with Conor since he returned the feeling. I am not sure how many pictures Conor actually took of Lucky before she finally curled up in a ball in her little bed and went to sleep. Although she is getting bigger, she is still a little dog with the most adorable face and curly black fur.

As we open a bottle of wine, Conor begins to tell us all about his adventures traveling. I tell him how close I have become to Aunt Elsa and how I love listening to her stories of traveling. I really want to tell him about this house and why we moved here, but I know that I am not allowed to, or the magic may not work. I do tell him about our struggles to have a baby and how we are looking into becoming foster parents as well as starting the process of in-vitro. Ryan excused himself, saying he was tired, but I think he just wanted to give us time alone.

After another glass of wine and more conversation, I can tell he is tired, so I show Conor to the guest room and add, "Stay up as late as you want. The TV won't bother us."

"I am actually going to look at the pictures I took of Lucky. I bought a frame for Ryan with the intention of getting a good picture to give him for his birthday. Can I borrow your car in the morning to get it developed before I help get ready for the party?"

"Of course, I was going to tell you that you could use my car all week, and I will use Ryan's since he takes the train to work now," I say and add, "We really don't have much to do for the party tomorrow. It's going to be small."

"Thanks, Tara," Conor says as he hugs me goodnight.

"Night, see you in the morning. I can leave the keys out, but I am sure that we will be awake before you now that we have Lucky to take out," I say as I close the door.

Ryan is still awake writing when I go into the bedroom, so I ask, "Are you doing the first task?"

"I finished it, actually. It is not as difficult as it seemed to think about those ages. The future was probably more difficult," he explains.

"I might work on mine before bed. I got sleepy when Conor and I were talking, but now I feel awake."

"Did you guys have a good talk?"

"Yep, I thought that's why you left. It's funny because I am the same person, but when all I did was work, we didn't have that much to talk about, but tonight the conversation just flowed."

"Was it hard not to tell him about this house?" Ryan asks.

"Yes, it was! Most of the time, it is okay, and I don't even think about telling people. I think because I can talk to Aunt Elsa and you, that helps, though maybe that is why it is hard not telling my mom since Elsa knows."

"Yeah, Conor was the first person I really wanted to tell. I think because we were talking about Lucky and our decision to get her," Ryan explains.

"It's almost your birthday. It's your last few minutes of being thirty-four," I say as I look at the clock and see that it is almost midnight.

"Wow, thirty-five, and you turn thirty-four next month."

"How different our birthdays are this year," I say as I reach over to touch his arm.

"And how different our lives and even we are this year," Ryan responds as we kiss.

Saturday, August 8

"Happy birthday," I say as I walk into the kitchen where Ryan and Conor are having breakfast. I meant to get up earlier, but since I worked on imagining myself at the different ages, I stayed up later than I intended.

"Thank you," he replies as I give him a kiss while he continues eating.

"I hope that you don't mind, but I made Ryan a little birthday breakfast of French toast," Conor says, "There is plenty for you too."

"Thank you, I might have some, but I need coffee first. Did you sleep well?" I ask Conor, who is already showered and dressed. He has on a light blue short sleeve button-down shirt and navy shorts.

"I did, although I usually only need six or seven hours of sleep," he says.

"Wow, not me," I say as Ryan agrees.

"Could I borrow a car still? Just for a couple of hours," Conor asks.

"Sure, you can use mine," I say as I sit down to eat.

When Ryan and I get back from taking Lucky for a morning walk, I say to Ryan, "Want your gift when we get home or wait until tonight?"

"Are you kidding? Of course, I can't wait until later."

Conor is still out, so we sit in the family room as Ryan opens his gift. I got him a fancy watch that connects to the computer. "I figured since you are walking Lucky and to the train every day, you need a way to track your steps," I explain.

"It's perfect. You know that we can go for walks, just the two of us if you want sometimes."

"No, I like taking Lucky, and she loves it too."

"Okay, but let me know if you ever want to. I realized as I was reflecting on the now or present moment that even though I am working less, I spend a lot of time with Lucky, and I don't want you to think that you aren't important."

"That's sweet of you. I am glad that you, we, have Lucky. I am spending more time painting and even meditating, so I am glad you love spending time with her. I was actually thinking that after Conor leaves, I might try to reach out to some of my old friends to see if they want to do something. I realized that I still see their updates on social media, but once they started having children, and we focused on our careers so much, the lunches and Friday night outings just disappeared," I explained.

"I thought about the same thing when we were talking about inviting others today. Since I don't really hang out with them anymore, it would be weird to invite them. Maybe we should start reaching out again and see what happens?" he agrees.

"I think also once we started trying to have a baby, and it wasn't happening, it hurt to see them with their children, so maybe I let those relationships fall to the side on purpose," I add.

"Yeah, maybe me too. Our life felt so different from theirs."

"We still don't have a baby, but with Lucky and our new focus on living life instead of only work, maybe we would feel a connection with them again?" I say as Lucky runs out to greet Conor, who has just returned.

"I love you," Ryan says, "Let's get ready for the party."

"I love you too. It's going to be a great day."

The party is in full swing when Nicky arrives to walk Lucky. I make sure to tell him that the food should be ready when he gets back. He has blond hair that is usually pulled back into a low ponytail and striking blue eyes. Today his hair is down, and he looks like he dressed up a little for the party. He is younger than me, but I am not sure how old.

With Nicky, there are nine of us, so I think we should be able to squeeze in at the table. We thought maybe we could eat outside because we have a patio with a big table and chairs, but since it is so humid out, we spent most of the party inside.

I hear Nicky return with Lucky, so I walk to the front door to make sure that he is staying to eat when I see Conor looking at him. I stop in my tracks for some reason because I really see my brother for the first time. He is smiling at Nicky in a way that I never saw him look at another person. Lucky notices me and runs over, so then Conor and Nicky turn and look at me. I notice that it is as if a light went off in Conor.

"Conor, this is Nicky," I say to divert the awkwardness, "You are staying for Ryan's birthday dinner, right Nicky?"

I swear I see him look at Conor for assurance as he nods yes.

Food, laughter, and wine flow long into the evening after my parents, Aunt Elsa and Uncle Riyen, and Ryan's mom left. Ryan loved his gifts from me, my parents, Elsa and Riyen, and his mom, but he especially loved Conor's gift, which was a picture of Ryan and Lucky walking last night. I know that he is my brother, but he is a great photographer catching the right angle and light.

"I almost forgot, Ryan, I brought you a gift," Nicky says as he hands him an envelope.

As Ryan opens it, he laughs and says, "Can I use one of these free dog walks right now? I think I have had a little too much wine."

"I can walk, Lucky," I offer so that Nicky can keep talking to Conor.

"We can walk, Lucky," offers Conor as he and Nicky get up together.

"Yeah, it's your birthday. You and Tara relax," Conor says.

"And you don't even have to redeem a coupon," Nicky says, winking at Conor.

"Thank you!" Ryan laughs as he pulls me onto his lap.

Once they are gone, Ryan says, "This was a great party."

"It was," I add, wondering what is going on between Conor and Nicky while at the same time wondering how and why my brother kept this from me. I also question how I didn't know before.

Saturday, August 15

I wake at five in the morning and decide to watch the sunrise. When I was young, I can remember the times that my friends and I would race to the beach in the morning just to watch the morning start the day like this. When and why did I stop doing things like this? Living in the now rings through my brain. If I had woken earlier, I could have walked to the beach since it is only around three miles away, but instead, I grab a coffee and the keys and head out, trying not to wake Lucky, Ryan, or Conor.

I have been struggling the last two days since I once again had "a feeling" that I was pregnant that turned out to be wrong. I don't know why I convince myself that I feel so different and that maybe now it will happen naturally.

I still haven't asked Conor about his interest in Nicky because he went to my parents on Sunday after the party and stayed with them most of the week. I only saw him a few times when we met for dinner once and when he stopped by the house another day.

Last night, he invited Nicky to come out with us, so Ryan, Conor, Nicky, and I went out to dinner and a movie and then hung out when we got home. I am not positive, but it sounded like they have been talking and maybe even spent time together during the week. I don't know how to bring up the subject. I keep telling myself that if Nicky were a girl, I would be teasing Conor about dating our dog walker, so why am I hesitant to do that now?

Ryan and I completed and shared our lists on Sunday and then started the thirty days of looking for the gift of Now in each day. We realized as we talked through these exercises that Ryan gets stuck on the past, which makes sense because of his father dying when he was young. I get stuck in the future, believing that my real life won't start until I have a baby. I am trying to meditate for five minutes or more each day, asking God or the Universe to show me the gift of now each day, and that seems to be helping. Ryan said his ritual is trying to notice everything in his immediate environment when he walks Lucky instead of letting his mind wander to work or negative thoughts.

When I arrive at the beach and park my car, the sun is just starting to appear on the horizon. I take a video and some pictures but realize that they can't compare to what I actually see, so I put my phone away and sit down on the bench. The sun coming up reflects on the water, making it sparkle and glisten like diamonds. I stop and listen to the sound of waves crashing and coming onto shore and the birds singing their morning songs.

There is only one other person walking by the water, so I close my eyes feeling the warmth of the sun on my face. I know that I have been so frustrated these last couple of days about not being pregnant, but I feel a sense of peace as I sit here and watch this amazing sight. I know that it happens every day, and I just take it for granted.

Maybe tomorrow, Ryan and I will come to share this together. I sit for another thirty minutes before I get up to head home. When I drive up to the house, I see Nicky's car parked along the street. He and Conor walk out the front door holding hands as I pull into the driveway.

"Where were you?" Conor asks as I get out of the car.

"I just went to the beach to watch the sun come up," I say as I notice they aren't holding hands anymore. Is Conor afraid to tell me? Does he think I would judge him or be mad?

"Fun, we should do that tomorrow?" Conor says to Nicky with a smile.

Nicky nods, and I wonder what he thinks about Conor leaving tomorrow.

"Where are you guys going?" I ask.

"Just out to breakfast since I am leaving tomorrow. We are thinking of going to the Art Museum later if you and Ryan want to come."

"I will ask him. Is he awake?"

"No, but I did take Lucky for a short walk since she woke up when I got up," Conor says as they turn to leave.

"Let me know if you want to go, and we can pick you up later," replies Nicky as they get into his black jeep.

"Okay, have fun."

Even though I want to spend more time with my brother, we decide to stay home and let them go to the Art Museum together. Since it is Conor's last night here, we have plans with our parents for dinner. Nicky drops him off at the restaurant but doesn't come to dinner. Conor tells our parents that he went to the museum but never mentions Nicky, so neither does Ryan or me. Conor's flight is late morning, so he is staying with us again tonight; so as we drive home, I ask, "Is Nicky coming over tonight?"

"I am not sure. He doesn't want to infringe on our time together."

"It would not bother me. I like Nicky; invite him over if you want. What does he think about you leaving tomorrow?" I ask cautiously.

"We are trying to figure that out," he says.

"Well, if you two keep dating, maybe I will see you more," I tease.

He chuckles and doesn't deny it but doesn't confirm it, either. How can I know someone my whole life and not really see him? Was I so wrapped up in my own life that I didn't pay attention to my own brother?

"You know, Mom and Dad don't know?" he says quietly.

"I figured that since I just realized it when I saw you last Saturday."

"What do you mean last Saturday? We weren't even dating then."

"I saw when you first met Nicky. You didn't know I had just walked up, but your face was just glowing when you saw him. Then when you saw me, you put the mask back on. I am sorry, Conor, that I never really saw you before."

"That's okay. It's been a process of acceptance for me recently too. I didn't try to hide it, but I just struggled to accept it. I tried dating girls when I was young, but I just knew that I didn't feel the same about them that other guys did. The problem also was that I didn't really feel anything special for any guys either, until now."

"I love you," I say, not sure what more I can say.

"Love you too. I will text him if you two are sure."

"Yes," I said.

"Absolutely," replies Ryan.

"Thank you both," responds Conor with a smile as he types on his phone.

Sunday, August 30

It has been two weeks since Conor left and three since Ryan turned thirty-five. Conor and Nicky did go see the sunrise together after staying up all night talking. Ryan and I went to bed around one after telling Conor goodbye before Nicky took him to the airport. I didn't ask for details about how they will stay together, but Conor hinted that he might be back for Thanksgiving.

I still haven't reached out to any of my old friends because I want to figure out how not to feel jealous of their lives if we meet up. I am still meditating, trying to live in the present moment, walking, and painting. Ryan and I even planned a short trip to Lake Willis to celebrate my birthday in September. I really do love this life Ryan and I have together; I know I just need to stop thinking that it will really be perfect once I get pregnant.

We have another doctor's appointment next week with the fertility specialist, in addition to filling out the application to be foster parents, possibly. We will complete this step before we leave for vacation. We might just take that time off, open the next envelope that morning before we leave, or bring it with us. We haven't decided.

Ryan didn't live close to the beach growing up, so he never went to watch the sunrise. We have gone twice now. He agreed that it is beautiful and that we should come here more often. When we woke Lucky to go today, I think that she thought we were crazy getting her up before the sun even was up and getting in the car to drive somewhere. We decided to walk there last time to see how long it would actually take, but it is hard to get up that early on the weekend.

I just finished my first painting, and am thinking of starting one of the sun rising as I clean my brushes and put them away.

"What a beautiful flower," Ryan says as he looks up from reading.

"Thank you, I think it is done," I say, staring at it again. I focus on the present moment when I paint and realize I am peaceful and joyful while I do it.

We have eleven days left of this step, but I could see myself continuing this like I have made meditating part of my life.

Thursday, September 10

I order a drink at the bar while I wait for Ryan to get here for dinner. Since I worked from home today, I walked Lucky before I left. We decided to meet here to talk about the step we just completed. We did it; step five is complete. We leave for vacation tomorrow, and my birthday is in less than a week. I understand more how important it is to appreciate where I am today. I still struggle with my vision of what I thought my life would be like when I turn thirty-four, but I am so grateful for where my life is compared to where it was when we started on this journey back just six months ago in March.

Ryan texts that he missed the train, so he will be a little later as an older gentleman sits beside me, ordering a glass of water. Suddenly, this man just starts saying things out loud, maybe to me or just maybe to the universe.

"I am a nice guy."

"I had ice cream today."

"I couldn't wait any longer for her to show up."

"My wife died three years ago."

"I own my place. No more renting for me."

"I am working six days a week right now."

"Everyone loved my wife."

"My name is Ken."

"I have four TVs."

"I forgot my cell phone at home."

"There are three women interested in me."

"One woman put me under her spell. She asked me for money, so I gave her $100. Now I am behind in my bills."

"I have my own car."

At first, I felt annoyed. I just wanted to sit and relax until Ryan came. I look at my phone and nod or say, "Hmm" to some of his statements. After about twenty minutes of ignoring him, I realize that I am not being a kind person. This man isn't asking me for anything;

I am in a safe environment. I look over at him and just realize that maybe he is lonely. We talk a little as I sip my wine. I warn him not to give that person money if he can't afford it. I encourage him to visit his daughter and his mother.

When Ryan arrives, and I get up to leave, he thanks me for listening. I tell him to take care, and I leave, realizing that it really doesn't take much just to be nice. I often think about and say that I want to make a difference in this world. I want to encourage and inspire others, but what does that really mean? I keep looking for the perfect place to help others, but maybe I just need to start where I am at, even if it is only in little steps or small ways. I told Ryan what happened when we sat down, and although he was nervous that I was engaging with a stranger, he understood my point.

Then after talking this through and going over of the items we needed to do in this last step, we decide to pack the dream book and envelopes so that if we choose to open the next envelope on vacation, then we can. We will keep our options open and do what feels right.

Friday, September 11

We arrive in Lake Willis at three o'clock and check into the Bed &
Breakfast. We booked a sunset dinner cruise, so after unpacking, we
head to the dock. The sky is a perfect shade of blue, with not a cloud
in sight. The air is warm but not too hot or too cold since it is almost
fall. We settle into our seats as the boat pulls away.

"Do you think that Lucky is fine?" Ryan asks for the second time.

"Yes, your mom was happy to take her. She promised to call if there
are any issues."

"I know, but we never had a dog growing up?"

"True, but you do great with Lucky. I am sure your mother will
too. We also gave her Nicky's phone number if she needs help."

"We should have had Nicky watch her. He could have stayed at our
house with her," he says suddenly.

"I don't know why we didn't think of that, but your mom wanted
to watch her, and she seemed excited to help."

I haven't talked to Nicky about his relationship with my brother, and I
really still don't know that much about him, but I know that if my brother
likes him, he must be a good guy. Conor told me that they text every
day and try to chat via video every week but that he misses him. He is
busy traveling and taking pictures because once Ryan suggested animal
magazines and sites, the demand for his photography skills have increased,
in addition to families wanting him to take professional pictures of their pets.

"Maybe I should text her to check?"

"Okay, should I order you a glass of wine?" I ask as I see the waiter
coming.

"Sure," he replies.

After Ryan is reassured that Lucky is sleeping peacefully, we enjoy a
wonderful dinner as the sun is disappearing into the lake. We make the
short walk back to where we are staying and get ready for bed. Ryan says

72

that tomorrow is the day for me to choose whatever I want to do since it is my birthday celebration. My actual birthday is Tuesday, but we will be home by then. I am not sure what I want to do, but I all I can think about is the next envelope. I thought maybe I could forget about the magic of the house and our dream just for a few days, but I am really enjoying the challenges these envelopes give us. I have grown and changed so much in these six months that I just don't want to wait another minute.

"Do you think that we should open the next envelope tomorrow?" I say as we are falling asleep.

"I was thinking the same thing, but since it's your day, I didn't want to say it," Ryan replies as he holds me, and I fall asleep in his arms.

Saturday, September 12

When I awake, the first thing that I smell is the coffee that Ryan brought up from the kitchen to start our day.

"Morning, honey," he says as I open my eyes, noticing the book and envelopes sitting on the table next to him.

"Morning," I reply as I stretch and sit up. After a quick trip to the bathroom, I sit back next to Ryan on the bed.

"Let's read all of the previous envelopes and go through the book of dreams before opening the next one," I say as I hold the one with the words 'BEGIN' on the front.

Once we are done, Ryan hands me the envelope and says, "Since it's your birthday weekend, how about you read this one?" I smile as I open it and begin to read.

Congratulations on completing the fifth step of this adventure. Your last step is really a reminder. It is to "Remember the steps to making your dreams come true. They are simply to BEGIN."

B=Believe
E=Examine
G=Gratitude
I=Intention
N=Now

You are ready to make your dreams come true since you are reading these words. There is no time limit to this step since different dreams take different amounts of time to manifest. You should continue to believe in the magic of this house, examine your life to ensure that the choices you are making align with your dream, and always begin each day in gratitude. Be thankful for this journey, be clear with your intentions, and live in the present moment of now.

Review these steps each week, and whenever you feel that you are not sure about a step or envelope, you should revisit those exercises and complete them again. At this point, it is important that you take action because your dream won't come true just by wishing; however, I can't give you the steps to take or the exercises to perform. You must decide what they are and then do them. It is time to discern what your next steps are on your own, to know what your truth is. It takes courage; it requires action, and it needs love. While still holding your dream in your heart, you must also release it. See where your life is leading you, and trust that path. Listen to your intuition, to that little voice guiding you and helping you.

This little stone house contains the remarkable power to make your dreams come true, but in order to manifest your dreams, you will need to continue to believe, as well as take these necessary steps along the way. Remember also, as it will be with all steps, you cannot read ahead; each envelope must only be opened when the current exercise is completed, and you must not tell others what these envelopes say unless and until it is their turn to have their dreams come true. This is your last step, but not your final envelope. Do not open the next envelope until your dream is a reality.

"Maybe we should have waited until after our vacation to open this one," Ryan says sadly when I finish reading.

"Yeah," I reply, thinking about the contents of this step, "I thought it would be something concrete to do. This is more difficult since we have to actually figure out what to do next."

"Maybe we just get on with the day celebrating you, just focusing on today and on the gift of this present moment," Ryan suggests.

"I agree. Let's go look at some bookstores," I say.

"And get some fudge," Ryan laughs as I get up to get ready.

I try to stay in the moment of now and forget about the magic house, the book, the envelopes, and having a baby as we walk around town looking at the art galleries, bookstores, and the other little shops.

Some of them remind me of the store back home, as I look for a souvenir from this trip. After a quick lunch, we buy some delicious chocolate fudge and then head back to relax in our room.

"Want to go workout before dinner?" Ryan asks when we get back to the room.

"I think I am just going to relax and read a little, but I don't care if you go. We have plenty of time."

I fall asleep reading, and by the time I wake up, Ryan is back from working out and done showering.

"How was your workout?" I ask groggily.

"Good. Did you want to go out for dinner or eat here?"

"Let's go down to that place by the lake so we can watch the sunset," I suggest, "I will get ready quickly so we can get a table before it gets crowded."

"Okay."

"I should have brought my paints," I say as the sky changes colors in the distance while we eat our steak nachos.

"Why don't you take a picture to use later and try to paint it at home?"

"Good idea," I reply as I snap a couple of the sky and then ask our waiter to take one of us.

As we are finishing the meal, Ryan hands me a box and says, "I saw this today. Your real birthday gift is coming Tuesday, but I thought you would like this."

Once I unwrap it and open it, I see a gold bracelet with the word DREAM on it, and I get up to hug Ryan as a tear wells up in my eye, "Thank you, Ryan. I love it."

Ryan has always been practical and frugal with money, so I know that it took a lot for him to buy a souvenir bracelet for me.

As if reading my mind, he says, "I hope you like it. I know I usually don't go for the sentimental stuff, but I am realizing that little moments like this are really the big things in life."

"I agree, and I do love it. I know we weren't going to think about the envelope today, but this can be one of the things we do," I say.

"What do you mean?" he asks as I sit back down.

"We can look for the little things, look for the important things each day or maybe each week."

"I like that, maybe each week, to reflect back. Maybe since we read the envelopes on Saturdays and Sundays, we could have a reflection day on either of those days, every week," Ryan suggests.

"Yeah, maybe Sunday since it's a nice thing to focus on before we start the next work week."

"So, do we start tomorrow?"

"I don't know. Let's let our feelings and intuition guide us when we wake up, but right now, let's get just enjoy the view," I laugh as I slip my new bracelet on.

Monday, September 14

Since it was raining when we woke up yesterday, we decided to pull out the envelope again to see if there was something that we were missing. After reading all of the steps again, and even meditating together, we decided that we could spend time every Sunday focusing on the five steps so that we could let our instincts guide us. We both loved Ryan's idea about looking at the little things in life because we have really come to understand that those little things are what matters. We love when we take the time to go out together for dinner or even for a walk. Ryan cherishes his time with Lucky, and I know that meditating and painting are an important part of my life now.

We will still use our gratitude jar, in addition to keeping a list of the little things in our lives. We also want to create a reminder to keep these five steps alive in our feelings, thoughts, and actions. I decided that I am going to paint a sunrise picture next, instead of the sunset, as a reminder of the steps BEGIN since each day is another opportunity to make our dreams come true. Ryan wants to make little cards with the word BEGIN on them to keep at his desk and in his pocket as a constant reminder. I told him that I would like a card too, and he said that when I finish my painting, he could add a small print of it to the other side of the card. As soon as we came up with these ideas, the sun started shining brightly, so we went for a hike on the nearby trail. We also found a place that would allow us to bring Lucky with us if we decide to plan a little trip here again.

We had dinner at the bed and breakfast and spent time walking around on our last night here. I still can't believe that we spent so much time working and never made time for these vacations and little getaways. Even though it has only been a few months, it seems like a lifetime ago.

As soon as we got home today, Ryan raced to his mom's to pick up Lucky. I am finishing unpacking and starting laundry when I hear Lucky run down the basement stairs to me. I reach down to pet her chin as she licks me; I say to her, "Hello, Lucky. Did you miss me?"

"Yes, she said, 'Never leave me again,'" Ryan laughs as he comes down the stairs too.

I laugh along but notice that he looks like he might have been crying, which Ryan never does, so I ask him, "You were gone awhile. How was your mom?"

"She was good; we had a great talk. I told her about my new insight into the fears I have about dying and how my Dad dying so young affected me in ways that I wasn't even aware of."

"Wow, that's good. How was she about it?" I ask cautiously since I know that he always felt like he shouldn't talk about his father's death because he didn't want to remind her of it or upset her.

"We can talk about it more at dinner, but she told me she never talked about his death because she didn't want to upset me. Isn't that ironic that we both wanted to talk about him and his death all of these years, but were both afraid to upset the other one?"

"That is. I am anxious to hear about your talk, but I am not sure what we have in the refrigerator to make."

"I actually picked up pizza on my way home because I figured we needed to shop, and I didn't want to leave Lucky to go out since we just got home."

"And since you missed her so much," I tease.

"Didn't you? I mean, don't get me wrong, I had a wonderful time at the lake, but it's good to be home."

"I did miss her. I love when our little family is all together. Let's go eat that pizza," I say as we head upstairs.

As we eat dinner with Lucky at Ryan's feet, Ryan tells me more about his talk with his mom. When he explained to his mom that he has a deep-seated fear about becoming a father because of his dad dying, his mother told him that his father was struggling with high blood pressure and high cholesterol for the last few years of his life. Even though he was young and appeared to be in good health, he worked long hours and most likely had a genetic disposition for these things. She also explained that since he didn't like the side effects of the pills that the doctor prescribed for him, he took himself off of them and was trying to eat healthy and exercise. While they will never know for sure, that might be why he had a heart attack and died so young. She also revealed to him that his dad thought he could work hard now and then have time to travel and spend more time with his family.

"That is interesting," I respond, "You always thought your father just enjoyed his job more than being with you and your mom, but really he wanted to work hard so that he could have time later with you both."

"Yeah, sort of like how I was living life before we moved. The more I talked to my mom, the more I realized that I really didn't know my father that well. I just made assumptions about him and never dug deeper. Then when he died, that took away any chance of getting to know him better."

"Both of us were doing that. I am so happy that you were able to talk to your mom about this and that you realized that you had these fears."

"Me too. I am definitely going to schedule a physical and tell the doctor about the family history to make sure that I do all that I can to stay healthy," he explains.

"Maybe we need to start thinking about the changes we can make together in our diet and exercise habits," I offer, "Like less pizza, maybe."

"True, I am going to spend more time with my mom too. I guess there is much I assumed about her, too," Ryan says, lost in his thoughts.

"That would be nice," I answer, thinking that I should reach out to my mom, dad, Aunt Elsa, and Conor.

"Plus, she said Lucky is welcome at her place any time," he laughs.

"Wow, she must have behaved well all weekend," I say as she looks up at me with her tail wagging.

"Of course she did," Ryan says as he bends down to pet her, "You were such a good girl, weren't you?"

Tuesday, September 15

"Have a good day at work," I mumble as Ryan walks out of the bedroom.

"I didn't mean to wake you. Happy Birthday," he says as he comes back to kiss me.

"Thank you," I say as we kiss.

"I can walk Lucky, so she should be good, and you can sleep more."

"Okay, I am meeting my mom for lunch, and then I am going to start my sunrise painting," I say as I roll over.

"Sounds like a fun day. I will leave work earlier than usual. I can't wait for dinner and for your surprise."

He has been teasing me with a so-called surprise all week, but I have no idea what it could be. I drift back off to sleep, wondering what the surprise could be.

After sleeping in, I just finish meditating and am getting ready to walk Lucky when my phone rings.

"Hello, Mom," I say as I answer.

"Happy birthday," she says, "Ready to meet for lunch?"

"I still have to walk, Lucky, but then I am ready. I wanted to stop and get another canvas and some more paints today too."

"Are you painting another flower? I loved the last one you did."

"No, I am going to try a sunrise picture," I say, almost explaining that I am doing it as a reminder of the BEGIN steps, suddenly remembering that she doesn't know about them or the secret of this house. I need to ask Aunt Elsa how she was able to keep it a secret. Sometimes I forget.

"That will be pretty, I bet," she replies.

"Did Aunt Elsa want to come for lunch?"

"No, she said that she and Uncle Riyen are coming to dinner, though."

"Okay," I answer as I put the leash on Lucky, "I am going to walk her now. Do you want to meet me at that shop in town?"

"Do you mean Manifest?" she asks.

"Yes," I say, realizing that I never paid attention to the name of it, but it is a perfect name.

"How's the birthday girl," Ryan says as he walks in the door, and Lucky runs over to him.

"Good, but I didn't realize it was so late," I say as I look up from the canvas, "I better clean up."

"You have a little more time to paint. I came home early to walk Lucky before dinner. How was lunch with your mom?"

"It was nice, but she had to leave for some reason right after we ate, so I came home and started painting."

"It is looking good," he says as he looks at the canvas with just the colors of the water and sky starting.

"Thank you," I answer.

"I made the BEGIN card today, but I really think I want a picture of your sunrise on the other side before I print and laminate them for us."

"Oh, the pressure is on," I laugh as he puts the leash on Lucky.

"Yep," he chuckles as they walk out the door.

When we arrive at the restaurant, I see that the surprise Ryan was talking about, and probably the reason my mom had to leave after lunch is my brother Conor. I know that it wasn't that long ago that he was in town, but I can't remember the last time that he was here on my birthday.

"This is the best surprise," I say as I give him a hug. I don't see Nicky, but since I am not sure what he has told my parents yet, I don't ask him. After hugging him, I also hug my parents, Aunt Elsa, Uncle Riyen, and Ryan's mom.

Because it has been such a rollercoaster few months of emotion, I get a little choked up at the end of dinner, opening presents, and having cake as I say to everyone, "Thank you all for helping me celebrate!"

Sensing the emotions I am feeling, Ryan comes over to give me a hug. I am so grateful for all that I have in my life and wish I could share with everyone the journey that Ryan and I are on.

"Well, you can't get rid of me yet. Ryan said that I can stay with you the next couple of days before I fly out," Conor says.

"You know that Nicky can come over tonight if you also want," I whisper as we hug.

"Thanks, sis," he whispers back.

"You can take some new pictures of Lucky, too," Ryan adds.

Sunday, September 27

"I am almost done," I tell Ryan as I put the final touches on my sunrise painting. Although I feel like I could still keep adding to it, I know that at some point, I need just to say that it is done. The perfectionist in me wants to keep improving it, but I know that the imperfections in it make it perfect. Even though this is the quickest I have completed a painting, Ryan was anxious to make our BEGIN cards so that we are constantly reminded of the steps to making our dreams come true.

In many ways, I feel that my dream has already come true even though we do not have a baby still. We just feel so much more like a family now; Ryan and I are close and connected in a way that I didn't even know was possible, and then Lucky just brings us so much joy. We discussed what steps to becoming parents feel right, so we are still working with the fertility specialist, but we are also looking into being foster parents. I do still want a baby, but I know that our family is already complete and that a baby or a child, if we end up becoming foster parents, will just be icing on the cake.

Each Sunday, we will sit together and review the envelopes and the dream book so that we continue believing in the magic of this house. We also know how important it is to examine and reflect on our lives and the choices we are making so that we don't fall into old habits. We need to be grateful, stay clear on our intentions, and live in the now.

We are still working out what actions we need to take since this envelope did not give us specific tasks to do. We often laugh when we think of how much our lives have changed since we moved here, but most importantly, we just try to be in the moment, appreciating where we are today.

I am still practicing meditation, but Ryan read about journaling, so he is trying that daily since he never enjoyed meditating like I do. Another thing we have started doing in the last couple of weeks is reflecting on what little things in life are really the big and important things. So far, these steps are enough, but I know that there are different actions we will be guided to take as time goes on.

After my birthday dinner, Nicky came over, and we stayed up late talking about everything. It turns out that Conor did not reveal his relationship with Nicky to our parents yet. Ryan told him that he could have him at my birthday dinner, but Conor told him that he needed more time before he told everyone. He has known since he was a young boy but tried to deny it until he met a guy in college named Matt. I keep trying to look back at our life growing up, but I think that Conor did a good job keeping this secret, maybe trying to keep it even from himself. That makes me sad, though, to think about having to hide who you are from those close to you. I guess that explains why he left for college and really never came back home.

Nicky told us that he came out to his mother when he was in high school and that she was more supportive of that than when he moved to California to try and become an actor. He doesn't really have a relationship with his father.

I told Conor that I would be there to support him when he is ready to tell our parents. Neither of us know how they might react when he tells them, but I would like to believe that it wouldn't matter to them, that they love and accept him no matter what. We talked again about how hard it has been with our struggles to have a baby. He said that he never knew because we both just seemed so focused on our careers and achievement.

I did tell him and Nicky about the changes Ryan, and I are making without revealing how and why we are doing it. I almost cried when he told me that he was proud of me for changing my life and that I seem so much happier now than I was when he used to come to visit. I was sad to see Conor leave since I feel closer to him now more than I ever have since we were little kids, but I know that we will be talking more often now than we did in the past.

Thursday, October 22

I am really enjoying the work-life balance I have now working from home. Unless I really need to go into the office, I try to work from home two or three times a week. Then since I don't have to commute to the office or spend time getting ready for being in the office, I start painting or reading when my workday is over. Also, because I am home more for Lucky, Ryan has been going to see his mom more often. They seem to be growing closer, which is good for both of them.

We both carry our BEGIN cards, and I even have one posted on the bathroom mirror. I brought my painting in to get framed, but I am not sure where I want to hang it, somewhere that I can see it and be reminded of every day. After finishing the sunrise painting, though, I went back to painting another flower; this time, it is an orchid. I am not sure why I am drawn to flowers, but I love the details I see in them. On the surface, flowers are so beautiful, but the inside characteristics are exquisite, sort of like my life now.

"Hi Tara, are you busy?" Nicky says when I open the door. For a minute, I think maybe I forgot to tell him that I was working from home and don't need him to walk Lucky, but then I realize that since he rang the doorbell, he knows.

"Of course. Come in," I say.

"So I know that it is short notice, but I can't walk Lucky this week after Tuesday. I could see if I can find anyone to come, but I wasn't sure if you would want that."

"No, I think Ryan and I can work it out," I offer.

"I'm actually going to Texas for Conor's birthday," he says without looking up.

"Oh, wow, that will be so much fun. I didn't know where he was going to be on his birthday since he is traveling so much lately," I say.

"I know, me too, but since it is his birthday, I want to celebrate with him," he explains.

Although I talk to Conor every week now, and I knew that he and Nicky are dating, I am still surprised to hear that Nicky is flying to Texas to see him for his birthday.

"It is his golden birthday. Conor is turning 28 on the 28th," I laugh.

"Yeah, I still don't know what to get him. I have been trying to figure it out even before I knew we were going to be together."

"I am sure that just having you there will be enough," I say as I realize that they must be getting serious. I knew that Conor had strong feelings for Nicky, but I wasn't sure how Nicky felt.

"Want to go for a walk with Lucky and me, so we can brainstorm together," I ask since I realize that if they are getting serious, I want to know Nicky better.

While we walk, I tell Nicky how Conor loved eighties music growing up. We also discuss that he loves old-style turntables to play his music on, so Nicky is going to find him a classic record. He also told me about how it was living in California for three years when he was trying to be an actor after college. He explains that even though he still wants to be an actor, his mother got sick, so that is why he came back home. He started dog walking because he always loved animals and thought it would give him some flexibility to be with her.

"She is doing better now, but I am not sure if I will go back to California for acting. I am involved with the little Playhouse community here in Walton," he explains.

"Oh, I didn't know that."

"It is a great group of people," he says.

"They have small workshops and events all year round, but the next big production is in the spring."

"When are tryouts for it?" I ask.

"Tryouts are actually in a couple of weeks," he says with so much excitement.

"Well, you will have to let Ryan and I know, so we can come to see you," I say.

"I mean, I didn't even try out or get a part yet," he laughs.

"I bet you will, though; I just know," I say.

I call Ryan after Nicky leaves to tell him about next week and about our conversation. He is surprised, too, that they are that close, but he says that really likes Nicky.

"Did you ever think that Conor was gay?" I ask.

"I never did," he answers.

"I didn't either, which makes me sad that I didn't."

"Tara, Conor didn't want anyone to know. Just be grateful that you know now. Remember that you don't want to hold the burden from the past," Ryan answers.

"I know. I want to go see Aunt Elsa when I am done working today to see what she did for this step, to maybe get more insight into what actions we should be taking. Also, to ask how she kept it a secret from everyone."

"Okay, good idea," he says, "I should be home to walk Lucky and make dinner."

"I will be home by six-thirty. Love you," I say as we hang up, and I call Aunt Elsa.

Sunday, December 6

"I can't believe that it has already been almost three months since we read this envelope," I say as we sit on our bed, looking at the little corner we just finished creating in our bedroom. We decided to keep the dream book and the envelopes in a special spot in our bedroom so that we don't forget the magic of this house.

Last week, we purchased a little corner table with a drawer at Manifest that has a dark red colored cloth on it and some other inspirational items we have purchased to remind us of the steps. We did hang my sunrise painting in the kitchen but framed our vision boards and hung them on the walls above the table as a constant reminder of this journey. In the drawer are the book and envelopes with the last one that we haven't opened on top that simply states, 'Only open when your dreams have come true.'

"And that it's been almost eight months since we moved here!"

"Yeah, sometimes it seems like we have lived here forever, yet it also feels like it was yesterday," I laugh.

"I still can't believe we sold the condo?" Ryan asks.

"I didn't really see us living there again. Do you regret it?" I ask.

"Not at all. I am just so surprised how different our life is."

"True, do we want to do our Sunday meeting and reflection now?"

"Sure, but let's take Lucky for a walk first."

As we walk, I think about the reminders of BEGIN that we created, like this corner in our bedroom, the little cards Ryan made, and my sunrise painting. I still continue to meditate, and Ryan has continued journaling since he found that more helpful. He does one page of longhand, free-thought writing a day.

"Want some water?" I ask Ryan when we get home.

"Sure, can you grab me an apple, too?" he says from the bedroom. I cut up a couple of apples and bring them and the water into the bedroom, where Ryan has the dream book and envelopes out already.

"Maybe we need two chairs in the corner too?" I say as I sit on the bed next to Ryan and Lucky.

"There might be room for two small ones," Ryan says as he looks at the corner.

We finish our weekly ritual of reviewing the envelopes and the dream book and then reflecting on whether we need to repeat any of the steps. Next, we discuss what little things were really the big and important things this week. It has been challenging not having the letter tell us exactly what to do, but we realize that it takes time for dreams to come true because once you set your intention, there are a series of individual things put in motion that need to occur first.

Like with any goal people have, there can be things that help or hinder achieving it, so we started an action step book last month. It may change, but we decided to do this on the first Sunday of each month. It is a simple, little start, stop, and continue exercise. We write down what steps we should continue to take toward our dream, what steps we should start toward our dream, and ask if there is anything we need to stop doing that might be preventing or blocking our dream.

"I think it's time that I finally reach out to some old friends from college and maybe even high school. I know that I said I was going to before, but I think it is time," I say, "Maybe I will start with Alicia, my best friend from high school. She doesn't live that far."

"So we can put that down for something for you to start," Ryan says as I write it in our action journal.

"It could even be considered something I need to stop doing, like stop avoiding old friends who have kids," I say more to myself.

"True. I was thinking maybe I would look into opening my own law practice as an action step. I would love more of a work–life balance."

I know that learning about his father's health conditions has really influenced Ryan's decisions. When he confronted his fear of dying young like his father, we made the decision to get healthy. He had already been lifting weights, but now he is running in addition to walking Lucky every day. He is envious that I can work from home two or three days a week and wishes that he had more flexibility. I know that ever since Lucky became part of our life, the daily commute feels worse than before since he is excited to get home.

"I think that would be a good action to take," I reply as I again look over at our vision boards, thinking that maybe our original dream is changing and expanding.

> *"Only open when your dreams have come true."*

Monday, April 18
(Two years after moving to the little stone house on the corner)

As I lay next to Bella until she falls back to sleep, I whisper to her, "We knew the first moment that we saw you staring up at us with those big brown eyes that you were ours, and we belong to you, just like I feel your brother or sister moving and growing inside of me does. I love you so very much; you are safe here, always know that."

I am not sure that she understands the words that I am saying, but I know that she can feel Ryan's and my enormous love for her. I don't know the pain and suffering she experienced before she came to live with us and became part of our family, but I do know that I could not love her more if she came from my own body.

"Did Bella sleep through the night?" Ryan asks as I crawl back into bed.

"She only woke once a little bit ago, but I was able to calm her down and get her back to sleep, and it didn't even take that long this time."

"That's good. She's getting better and learning that we will always be there for her," Ryan says as he holds me a little tighter.

"Do you know what today is?" I ask.

"Umm, Monday, so I have to go to work?" he answers.

I took a short leave from work since Bella became a part of our family to help her adjust, but I do miss working, especially with the flexibility of working from home some days. I am not sure what we should do once the new baby arrives too, but we have a little time to figure it out. I will trust the universe to guide me to the highest good for our family.

"Yes, but it is also the two-year anniversary of the day that we moved here."

"Wow," he responds, as I realize that I can barely remember our life without Bella, Lucky, and this wonderful little stone house on the corner.

"Ryan, I think we should read the final envelope," I say as I kiss him.

He replies, "That day is here for sure. My dreams have come true."

"Should I go get it now or wait until after you get home from work?"

"Let's wait until Sunday. We can just enjoy the rest of this week first," he suggests.

"Good thinking. You never know what we might have to do once we read it," I respond wondering what it will say.

"I guess it is time to add ours to the dreams that have come true book too."

"Yes, indeed," Ryan says as we hear Bella waking again.

Sunday, April 24

Ryan reads the front of the envelope first that says, *"Only open when your dreams have come true."*

"Do you want me to read it?" I offer even though Bella is sitting on my lap.

"I can," he says as he unfolds the paper and begins to read.

Congratulations, and always remember the steps to making your dreams come true. Now that yours has come true, you are ready to share the gift of this house with another person. Keep your intentions clear and your expectations open to see whom this house leads you to. Trust the process, and you will not go wrong.

I know that you are afraid to move, fearful that you won't be able to make your dreams come true away from this house but believe me when I say that you can. You just need to follow the five steps, BEGIN. Even though it is time for you to pass on the gift of this house to another, the true gift of this house is the learning and the knowledge about how the universe of dreams creates and manifests. Somehow believing that the power is contained in this special house is easier than believing in your self.

When I moved into this little stone house on the corner, I knew this house was something special even though the windows were so dirty I could barely see through them the first time I saw it. I also knew that my dreams would come true, not because I moved here, but because I believed that they would. It wasn't simple, nor was it easy, but it was possible and is possible for everyone.

The envelopes show the steps I discovered to create and manifest, and the book of dreams gives us the faith to trust in the power. We each hold the power of creation within us, but sometimes we need a little reminder. That is what this little stone house on the corner does; it reminds us of who we are.

Bella moved to the floor to pet Lucky as Ryan read, so I move closer to him as he finishes to see if there is more.

"Wow is all I can say," Ryan says as he touches my hand.

"I can honestly say that I did not see that coming. I think I need to read it again," I say.

"Me too. Read it out loud," he says as hands me the paper and moves to the floor with Bella and Lucky.

"I still think this house is magic," I say after reading it again.

Then as I fold the paper and put it back into the envelope, I ask, "Want to go out for breakfast?"

"Sure, I can take Lucky out while you get Bella ready."

"Lucky," says Bella as I pick her up.

"Yes, we are, Bella," Ryan chuckles even though he knows that she was saying Lucky's name.

"Daddy will be back with Lucky soon," I tell her.

"Daddy," she says for the first time.

"Tara, did you hear that? My sweet girl called me daddy," Ryan chokes up as he walks over and gives her a kiss. Since I have been home from work since Bella came to us, she has said Mommy much quicker. I try to talk to her about Ryan often, even pointing to his picture during the day, but I know Ryan was anxious to hear her call him that.

"I did, honey," I respond, "Do you want me to walk Lucky, and you can get Bella ready?"

"That would be great," he says as he takes her from me. Even though she is almost two years old, she is very small for her age. I know we should try and stop picking her up all the time, but we both keep forgetting.

Sunday, May 1

"I really do love this community," I say as we walk from the car. Bella is walking, holding Ryan's hand, so we are moving slowly.

"Me too. It is hard to believe that we have only lived here for a little over two years. It really does feel like home to me," Ryan agrees.

"Even though we haven't figured out who should move into the little stone house on the corner, maybe we should start looking for a bigger house anyway?" Ryan suggests.

"True, I don't want to leave this house, but it probably is time for us to take that next step."

"I really like the area Alicia lives in. It's not too far from here, and the schools are good there," I say, adding, "Although we wouldn't be as close to town or the beach from there."

It was difficult to reach out to Alicia, but once I did, we are almost as close as we were back in high school. We grew apart when we went off to college, and then even more once I was a few years into my career, and she quit work to stay home to start a family. She never felt hurt because, in many ways, she distanced herself from me by making new friends who also had children. Talking to her made it easier for me to reach out to some of my college friends to reconnect too. Ryan and I still don't have a lot of time for friends, but we have both made more of an effort to go out with people at work for more family and health-friendly outings.

"We could also look around here, too," Ryan says.

"Maybe once we start looking for a new home, we will know who should move into the little stone house," I say.

"I actually have an idea for someone," Ryan says quietly.

"You do? Why didn't you tell me?" I say excitedly.

"I am not sure if you will agree; plus, I am not sure what this person's dream will be."

"I don't think we need to know. Everyone has some dream. It was just easier, maybe for Aunt Elsa, since she knew our dream," I offer.

"Or maybe that makes it harder since she really wanted it to come true."

"Maybe, so who is it?" I ask, thinking about what Ryan said.

"Nicky," Ryan answers.

"Like Nicky, our dog walker; like Nicky, Conor's boyfriend?"

"Yes, that, Nicky," Ryan laughs.

"As you said, I am not sure about his dream and if it would include my brother or if it would be his old dream to be an actor. I think he is a good idea. Why did you think I would say no to him?"

"I didn't necessarily think you would say no, but I thought he would make it complicated. Would we want his dream to be an actor to come true since maybe he and Conor would break up, or what if he thinks we are crazy suggesting this house is magical and breaks up with Conor over it?" Ryan says.

"I didn't think of that. I wonder if Aunt Elsa had that fear?" I say, thinking about how often I turn to her to ask questions about what this journey was like for her. She didn't keep in touch with the person who sold her the house, so she didn't have someone to ask.

I remember when I went to her to talk about the last step and how frustrated we were that there were no concrete actions to take; she told me to just trust the process. She never told us what to do and even tried to not influence our decisions at all. She moved into the little stone house alone, so she also couldn't talk to someone like Ryan and I can with each other. She thinks that since she did it alone, that made it easier to keep the secret from everyone. Maybe she is right since Ryan, and I talk about the steps and the envelopes all of the time, and we both struggle not to tell others what we are doing.

Only Aunt Elsa knew her dream, but she did tell Uncle Riyen when they got married since he was moving into the house too. She thought maybe he had a dream he wanted to come true, but he told her that his dream had already come true on the day they met. They lived there together for a year before she felt guided to us moving into the house.

I am grateful that Ryan and I went on this adventure together and that we were able to grow closer through it.

As if he was reading my mind, Ryan responds, "I am glad we had each other."

"Me too. Let's both think about it and then decide, but I do think Nicky feels like the right choice," I say.

"Do you think it is too early to leave Bella with your mom to go see Nicky in the spring play?" I ask as I see the small community playhouse in the distance.

"She seems to be doing really well for the short times they have spent together," Ryan says, "Remind me of the date when we get home so I can ask her."

"We could also leave the play early if she has a hard time," I say.

91

"True," Ryan agrees. Nicky had a small part in last years play, but this year, he got the lead. Conor came for it last year, so I assume he might come again, especially since Nicky has a big part. I wonder what Conor would think if Nicky moves into the house. We have grown closer these last couple of years; however, Conor is still a very private person. I try not to ask him too many personal questions, but I am curious about how serious their relationship is and if they will stay together.

"Where did you want to go first? Should we get coffee or go to the bookstore?" Ryan asks.

"Bookstore!" yells Bella happily before I can answer.

Saturday, May 14

Nicky texted us that he wanted to talk to us this afternoon. It has been one week since we told him that we want him to move here. Just like Aunt Elsa said to me, I had explained to Nicky that this is a special house. It is a little house on the corner made of simple stone where extraordinary things happen to those who live here. I worried he would think I was crazy when I added that it makes dreams come true, but he didn't laugh or run out the door. He just asked if he could think about it.

Since he cannot afford to buy the house, nor does he even want to own a house here, we asked him to just move in and pay us rent to cover the mortgage. Even though we will no longer live here, my heart feels full that we will still own it. We need a bigger house for our growing family, and I know that this gift must be passed on. Now I understand how difficult it must have been for my Aunt Elsa and Uncle Riyen to move out when we moved in.

Nowhere in the book or envelopes do the instructions state that we must know the next recipient of this gift's true desire. We know that he loves my brother, and we know he had a dream of being an actor when he lived in California two years ago. If he moves in, we do not know what his dream will be, but we do know that this house will change him and his life forever as it did ours if he lets it.

After Ryan gets back from walking Lucky, we make a quick pasta salad for lunch and read a couple of books to Bella together. Once I get Bella down for an afternoon nap, we still have a little time before Nicky arrives, so we decide to re-read the envelopes. The first time we read them, we had no idea who we should pass this house to. I am unsure what we will do if Nicky says no; I am just hopeful that he will take this gift. It feels right, and I can imagine him living here.

When Ryan gets up to answer the doorbell, I move the book and the envelopes back to our bedroom corner area until we hear if he wants to accept this gift.

"Hi, Ryan," I hear Nicky say when the door opens.

"Hey," replies Ryan.

I take a quick peek to make sure Bella is still sleeping. I remember my nervousness and excitement when Aunt Elsa asked us to move here. Did I truly believe this house was magic, or was I just hoping for a miracle? Nicky is smiling as we hug, but does that mean that he believes and wants to move in?

"So I have spent the last week thinking about your offer. I have two questions, though, before I answer?"

"Okay, what are they?" Ryan asks.

"Can Conor move in here with me, and if he does, can I tell him my dream?"

Ryan and I look at each other, and by the look on his face, he is as surprised as I am. When Conor left Walton for college, he never really came back except to visit. I did not think he ever would.

"I didn't know Conor wanted to move back here," I say.

"I am not sure that he does, but we do want to be together. When I told him about your offer to move to this house, minus the details about it being magical, he suggested living here together until we figure out our future. So I thought I would ask you," Nicky blushes.

Obviously, Ryan knew about the house, and we read the letters together, but our dream was intertwined. I know that it is not my place to know his dream, but I wonder if Conor does need to know about the magic of this house to live here. Or if we tell Conor, could they do the steps while each having their own dreams, or maybe their dream is the same? Maybe I am overthinking everything.

"I would think Conor could move in here, but I am not sure about the second question. What do you think, Ryan?" I respond, turning to look at Ryan, who has the same expression as me.

"I agree that Conor could live here. I know Elsa told Riyen about the house when he moved in, but she made her dream come true first," Ryan says.

"Wait, your Aunt Elsa lived here?" Nicky asks.

"She did before we moved in," I answer, not really sure what else I should reveal until I know if he believes in the house.

"While we think about that, are you saying that you do believe and want to live here?" Ryan asks.

"It's complicated because, yes, I do believe, and yes, I do want to move here, but I don't think I could keep the secret from Conor. I love him and don't want to keep something like this from him. I could just tell him it didn't work out to move here if you decided that I couldn't tell him, and there would be no hard feelings," Nicky explains.

"I think I know the answer, but Ryan and I are going to talk about it first, okay?" I ask.

"Of course," Nicky responds.

"So, what are your thoughts?" Ryan says when we walk into the bedroom.

"Let me read the final step again. Here it says to keep your intentions clear and your expectations open to see whom this house leads you to. Trust the process, and you will not go wrong," I say as I fold the paper and put it back into the envelope.

Without really discussing it, Ryan and I walk back out to Nicky, and Ryan says, "We just need to know you believe and that Conor believes since that is the first step."

"So I can tell him about the magic of this house?" Nicky says excitedly.

"You can. I am not sure how it will work if you both have different dreams, but that is up to you two to figure out, obviously, if Conor believes," I say.

"He is arriving here in about an hour, so I can ask him then," he says.

"He didn't tell me he was coming," I say excitedly.

"He just decided to talk to your parents about, you know, us. He thought that it was time. No matter if we moved in here together or not," he explains.

"I knew he didn't want to keep your relationship a secret anymore," I say, knowing that Conor felt bad and didn't want Nicky to think he was ashamed of him and their relationship.

"Do you want us to explain to Conor about the house?" Ryan asks, realizing that Nicky has a lot going on.

"No, but if he has any questions, we will call you," Nicky answers.

"Take all the time you guys need to decide, okay?" I say as he gets up to leave.

Bella wakes up right as Nicky is leaving, so I hug him quickly and say goodbye.

"Does this still feel like the right choice?" Ryan asks as he walks into Bella's room.

"It does. My head is just spinning from it all. I am glad that Conor is going to talk to my parents since, in addition to the magic of this house, I have had to keep that secret too, which has been hard."

"I wonder what Conor will say?"

"I know, me too. Are you hungry, Bella? Let's go get a snack," I say as I put her down so we can walk to the kitchen.

Sunday, May 15

Conor called last night to see if he and Nicky could come by in the morning. If he talked to my parents or if Nicky told him about the house, he didn't let on. I told him yes, and he just said he loved me and would see us around ten.

Bella and I are finishing a little art project when the doorbell rings.

"What's my Bella making?" Nicky says as he, Conor, and Ryan walk into the kitchen. She tells him it's a dog as she gives him a hug. Since she sees Nicky much more than Conor, she is shy with Conor when he says hi to her.

"Hi, Nicky. Hey brother," I say as I give him and Nicky hugs.

"So after my talk with Mom and Dad last night, I just want to say that yes, I do believe in magic," Conor says.

"So the talk went well with them, and I assume Nicky told you about this special house?" I say.

"Yes, and yes," he laughs.

95

"That is all great news, Conor. You can ask us any questions and take all the time that you need to decide," Ryan says.

"We don't need time to think, and our only question is, when can we move in?" Conor responds.

"Really?" I laugh.

"Yes," Nicky and Conor both say.

"I am so happy. I want to hear all about your conversation with Mom and Dad, too," I say.

"I am going to call my mom to see if she can come to watch Bella for a little bit so we can talk privately," Ryan suggests.

Ryan's mother has been so helpful with Lucky and Bella. Even though she doesn't live in this magical house, she has also changed so much these last couple of years also. She doesn't work or travel as much, and she and Ryan have grown very close.

"Good idea," I say, "Can you guys come back closer to dinner?"

"We can do that," Nicky and Conor say together.

Ryan runs to the grocery store after lunch to get stuff to cook for dinner. His mom is coming over around six to take Bella for a walk and then play with her until bedtime. Ryan did tell her that Nicky and Conor might be moving in here since she knows that we already put an offer in on a new house and might be moving in less than two months.

He said she did not seem surprised by the news of Conor and Ryan being together. I still haven't talked to my parents about Conor's conversation with them, but I am happy that it went well.

Bella is finishing her dinner when Ryan's mom comes. After hugs and a quick conversation, she is heading out the door with Bella when Conor and Nicky arrive.

"Let's just start off with these envelopes and the book before we sit down to eat," Ryan says right away as we sit down on the couch.

"Okay," Conor smiles.

I add, "Believing in this house is the first and most important step. You can have concerns and be skeptical, but do you really believe that this is possible?"

"Hey, I watched the two of you transform before my eyes. If I didn't believe in magic before that, the changes you two made would have convinced me," Conor explains.

Nicky opens the first envelope that says *Believing is a simple task that takes much effort* on the front and begins to read out loud.

Congratulations on embarking on an amazing adventure. This little stone house contains the remarkable power to make your dreams come true. The first step is often the most difficult, but be proud, for you have decided to take it. This is not a genie-in-the-bottle-type house. In order to manifest your dreams, you will need to believe, as well as trust, and take the necessary steps along the way. You cannot move to the next envelope, step two until you are living here. Now as you prepare for and complete the task of moving into this special house, remember that believing is a simple task that takes much effort. As it will be with all six steps, you cannot read ahead; each envelope must only be opened when the current exercise is completed, and you must not tell others what these envelopes say unless and until it is their turn to have their dream come true.

"Any questions?" I ask when he is done reading.

"Like we said earlier, our only question is, when are you moving?" Conor laughs.

"We actually put an offer in on a new house this week, and if all goes well, we should be moving there in July," Ryan says.

"I can look for someone to sublet my apartment and be able to move in then, too," Conor says.

"That was quick and easier than when Aunt Elsa told us about the house. Now let's eat then since that is done," I say, "We can open a bottle of wine to celebrate."

"I forgot Aunt Elsa lived here first. So Mom and Dad don't know about this house?" Conor asks.

"I mean, they know our lives changed living here, but Aunt Elsa and Uncle Riyen are the only ones that know since they lived here before us."

"Wow," Conor and Nicky reply at the same time.

"If you look in the book of dreams fulfilled, you will see our names and Aunt Elsa's. She only told Uncle Riyen when he moved in with her because she thought he was the next recipient of the house, but he said his dream had already come true when they met," I explain.

"That must have been hard not to tell anyone," Nicky says.

"You have no idea, but you will learn soon enough," Ryan responds, "But at least we had each other, and you guys will have one another. I don't know how your Aunt Elsa kept it a secret."

When Ryan's mom and Bella get back from their walk, we are doing the dishes and discussing the details of them moving in with the envelopes and book safely tucked back in our bedroom.

Saturday, July 9

The house is still quiet when I wake up, so I tiptoe to the kitchen to think before the day gets busy. Bella seems to be adjusting well to life with Ryan and me, and hopefully, she feels secure and loved. The adoption is proceeding, but not as quickly as I want, but she is already our daughter, no matter what the paperwork states.

Today is her birthday; she is turning two. We are having her birthday party with just family at home since celebrating in this magical little stone house feels right. We will be moving soon, and even though Nicky and Conor will still live here, we want to be in the place where our lives turned upside down and then right side up.

I know the last envelope said that it was our own power that made our dreams come true, but this house will always be special in my eyes. It is amazing to think that we had only lived here two months when Bella entered this world. We had just got Lucky, were thinking of hiring a dog walker and doing our gratitude jar. Talk about being grateful.

Although I don't believe that Bella had to go through so much trauma and pain in the first year and a half of her life to come to us eventually, maybe the reason is just the one we assign to things, like she needed us, and we showed up.

Before we even knew Bella was coming into our lives and when we came up with the actions for the last step, we discussed that it takes time for dreams to come true because once you set your intention, there are a series of individual things put in motion that need to occur first. It started with us moving here, Bella being born to someone else who couldn't take care of her properly, us getting Lucky, and then hiring Nicky. But Conor still had to come home to meet Nicky. Then us being blessed enough to become Bella's parents and now also being pregnant, all had to come together to create this amazing life we are now living.

I hear Bella call out to me, so I go get her, and then together, we go wake up her daddy to wish her a happy birthday.

"Happy birthday," she repeats to us, and I smile, knowing that it will be a happy one for her.

"Are you ready for your party, Bella?" Ryan asks as she hugs him.

When she says, "Lucky," I smile, knowing she is calling for her to climb into the bed with us, but I also smile because I know that we are so lucky to be her family.

Conor and Nicky are the first to arrive since they want to measure the rooms to see what furniture they should each bring. Surprisingly, or maybe not, Conor found someone to sublet his place for right when they can move in here. Nicky's mom is sad to see him move out but is thrilled that, at least for now, Nicky will live close by. I know soon we will be giving the book and the letters to Nicky and Conor, but we decided that we want to keep our special table to remind us daily to manifest our dreams, although I think we both need to make new vision boards for our new dreams.

We can't read the letters once we move, but Aunt Elsa said she made her own notes so that she would never forget the steps and could continue to create the life of her dreams. I know I will still need to make choices day by day but with a clear vision of our future dreams and goals. We have learned how to live with awareness, intention, and purpose. We are making decisions specific to who we are, not for others or even our own expectations, and that is something that I never want to forget.

Conor and Nicky keep asking me questions about the steps and envelopes, but I know their path might be different than ours. I am not exactly sure what kind of journey this house will take Nicky and Conor on, but it is not for me to decide. Our task is simply to pass on the gift of this magical little stone house on the corner. They will find their way to make their dreams come true, and I know it will be amazing.

THE END

The steps to make your dreams come true are to BEGIN.

Believing is a simple task that takes much effort.
Examine your heart and your life to see what you really desire.
Gratitude is where life begins and ends.
Intentions create reality.
Now is the moment. Live in this truth, not in the past or in the future.

One: "Believing is a simple task that takes much effort." Congratulations on embarking on an amazing adventure to make your dreams come true. The first step is often the most difficult, but be proud, for you have decided to take it. In order to manifest your dreams, you will need to believe as you take the necessary steps along the way.

Two: "Examine your heart and your life to see what you really desire." To make your dreams come true, you will need to continue to believe as well as now; you must spend time in self-reflection and deep awareness of the life you are living and the choices you are making. Experiences in life without examination can rarely offer meaning or purpose. You will determine if your dream is really in alignment with your life, your choices, and your actions. There are a series of questions and tasks that you must do over the next month, or however long it takes to complete these five items to examine your heart and life to determine your true desires.
- List three things that you would make come true if you could today.
- List two ways/actions (under each of the three things above) that you have taken to achieve this thing.

- Reflect on this process. Become aware of your wishes and actions of each one. Look back at the experience for connection and learning. "That was an amazing experience," or "I didn't handle that the way that I wanted to." Focus on your feelings as you reflect on an experience, person, or situation. Learn from it so that you don't repeat things you didn't handle well.

- Determine if the dream, or wish you say that you want to come true, is at the top of your list right now. Is there another wish you want first or more? Examine if there are steps you could still take toward all of your wishes.

- Write out a detailed description of what your day-to-day life would look like if this dream came true. As you reflect on this, see where your focus was. Did you feel excited, anxious, or hopeful? Were you dreading parts of it? Did you feel sad, mad, happy, surprised, or scared?

Three: "Gratitude is where life begins and ends." It is important to understand that life begins and ends in a state of gratitude. You will focus on this for the next six weeks, so that it becomes second nature for you to live in this state of being thankful. Your task is simple, each day at the same time, either when you rise or go to sleep, you must name one thing that you are grateful for. They cannot be repeated, and it must be a complete thought, not just one word. You can do this any way you see fit, yet it should be fun and bring you joy.

Four: "Intentions create reality." After six weeks of living in a place of daily gratitude, you should be feeling much lighter. Next you will learn that intentions create reality. Although that may sound like a simple truth, it is much more complex than it appears because often people are not aware of their intentions. Also, we shouldn't take anything personally since we create collectively as well as individually. Remember that you can't control everything that happens in life. Not everything happens for a reason; some things are just random events in a multi-creating universe. Although we can and do create individually, group intentions also assist as well as interfere with your individual ones. There are four questions to answer, but you should only do one a day.

Then there are also three tasks to complete. You can take longer than seven days but not less than.

- Card #1: Refer back to your exercise in step two. Examine your heart and life to determine your true desires. What were the three things that you would make come true if you could, and reflect on what actions you took to reach them? Did you remember them as you completed the six weeks of gratitude exercise, and are you still making steps towards them?

- Card #2: When do you feel alive and time just flies by? What makes you feel happy, and what makes you feel at peace? When are you most joyful?

- Card #3: What are you fighting or resisting? Are you spending more time fighting what you don't want in your life? Because, remember, that what you resist will persist because you are creating that by focusing on it.

- Card #4: Based on from envelope two, review your description of what your day-to-day life would look like if this dream came true and adjust it, if necessary, based on your answers to cards 1-3 and your gratitude practice that you did for the six weeks.

- Card #5: Today is a day of contemplation. Spend ten minutes in quiet meditation at least five times over the course of the day, releasing negative feelings out and positive feelings in with deep breaths, inhaling in with the good, out with the bad. If you are not able to do all five times, you must wait until a day when you are able. You can do this out in nature or in your home. You can close your eyes or use an item like a candle to stare at it. The purpose is to clear your mind of all thoughts and see what comes into your consciousness, to see the truth of self. Sometimes it is helpful to repeat a word or sound.

- Card #6: Create a vision board. You can use pictures or drawings or simply write words or sentences. It must be clear what you intend to create or manifest in your life. You can have expectations, but it is important to let go of how you achieve the outcome. Be certain of your intentions, not an outcome. This is not a dream board.

- Card #7: Now that you completed your vision board, and you are keenly aware of what you are focusing on, you will focus on the power of "I am" statements. All day or as long as it takes, you need to ponder the connection between behaviors and consequences. If I am happy, what is the consequence? If I am angry, what is the consequence? Once you feel confident in this connection between what you are being and the consequences, your task is to write out an "I am" statement. Then write it out again, but eliminate the last letter, then continue to write it out on the next line while eliminating another letter, and so on until you have one letter left. Once you finish writing, hold this paper in your hand and surrender your I am statement to the universe, and then burn it in a safe spot, watching the embers and smoke, with your statement, being released above.

Five: "Now is the moment. Live in this truth, not in the past or in the future." In order to live in the present, not in the past or in the future, you will start by imagining yourself at each age and the events that passed or that will happen (5, 10, 15, 20, 30, 40, 50, 60, 70, 80, and so on). Reflect on what you were or will be doing, thinking, and feeling at that age and time. Once this task is complete, think about putting everything, good and bad, that you experienced in the past in your right hand; then, imagine all of your dreams and plans that you have for your future in your left hand. Now hold both hands in front of you; feel how heavy your hands are becoming holding the burden of the past and future in today. Once you can no longer hold the weight of your hands, clasp them together to live in the 'Now.' For the next month, you must look for the gift of today, of the now. You must understand that you deserve joy and happiness today. This is more than gratitude. Instead, you need to see the miracle of life that each day presents to you and take action where appropriate. Please repeat the hand visualization activity if you struggle to stay in the present, or you can create your own ritual to help you. You must live in the now and stop focusing on the past and/or quit believing that you will only be happy once you have exactly what you want.

Six: "Remember the steps to make your dreams come true. They are simply to BEGIN."

B=Believe
E=Examine
G=Gratitude
I=Intention
N=Now

You are ready to make your dreams come true since you are reading these words. There is no time limit to this step since different dreams take different amounts of time to manifest. You should continue to believe that you can make your dreams come true, examine your life to ensure that the choices you are making align with your dreams, and always begin each day in gratitude. Be thankful for this journey, be clear with your intentions, and live in the present moment of now. Review these steps each week, and whenever you feel that you are not sure about a step, you should revisit those exercises and complete them again. At this point, it is important that you take action because your dream won't come true just by wishing; however, you must decide what the actions are, to know what is your truth, and then do them. It takes courage; it requires action, and it needs love. While still holding your dream in your heart, you must also release it. See where your life is leading you, and trust that path. Listen to your intuition, to that little voice guiding you and helping you.

The true gift of these steps is learning how the universe creates and manifests. Know that your dreams will come true because you believe that they can. It isn't simple or easy, but it is possible for everyone. Follow the steps and trust in the power of creation within each of us.

Have faith and remember who you are.

About the Author

Susan Marie Schulhof lives in the Chicagoland area, and *Little Stone House on the Corner* is her fourth book. She has her Master's Degree in Psychology from National Louis University and has worked in the Early Childhood Education field since 2001. She has been writing a blog on positivity since 2016 and loves to hike, read, and spend time with her family when she is not traveling for pleasure or work.

Printed in the United States
by Baker & Taylor Publisher Services